One More Day,
One More Tomorrow:

One Family's Journey Through Suicide

One More Day, One More Tomorrow:

One Family's Journey Through Suicide

by

Sue Ann and Bob Varner

TABLE OF CONTENTS

PREFACE

Every story has a beginning and an end. This is our story about our son, Eric Varner. The beginning: when he was born and his end: when he succumbed to suicide. This story is about joy, love, pain, heartbreak, and loss. It is about a family who tried desperately to find the medical help their loved one needed but failed in doing so. It is a story about a wonderful young man whose life ended way too soon. This is Eric's story.

It was important to us when writing this book that you not only hear about our struggle as a mother and father who lost their son, but to also hear that of Eric's whole family. Eric's suicide affected all of us and we want everyone who is contemplating ending their life to understand what it will do to those who love you and the pain that will come from losing you.

If you feel suicide is your only answer to life's problems, this book is for you. If you get nothing else from reading about our family's struggle to make sense of our son's need to commit suicide, please realize that there is help for you and ending your life is not the answer.

PLEASE, PLEASE CALL THIS NUMBER: 1-800-273-8255.

If you know someone who you are worried about that may be struggling with mental health issues and possibly having thoughts of committing suicide,

PLEASE, PLEASE CALL THIS NUMBER: 1-800-273-8255.

Our prayers are with you and we hope that you will understand the importance of giving your life one more day...one more tomorrow. May it console you to know that others care.

THE SUICIDE HOTLINE IS 1-800-273-8255.

Who We Are:

We are Bob and Sue Ann Varner. We live in a small town in Northern Missouri and we have three children: Eric, Chad, and Natalie.

If someone had told us when our three children were young that one of them would eventually kill himself or herself, we wouldn't have believed it. We would have told them they were crazy. Our children were the same as other children—normal, happy, and at times a handful. There were never signs that our oldest son, Eric, would develop problems that would eventually lead him to commit suicide at the age of 43.

We are sharing our grief and our struggles with the hope that by doing so, others who have experienced the pain of losing a loved one to suicide will know they are not alone. Those of us who have lost a loved one to suicide have all had the same questions and experienced the same guilt:

Was it our fault?

Was it something we did or didn't do?

Did they call out for our help and we weren't there?

For someone to end their life, they have to be experiencing tremendous pain. Whether that pain is physical, mental, or both. Occasionally, we may hear of someone who has committed suicide; sometimes it is a celebrity and sometimes it is the person who lives next door. We hear of these people and wonder:

Why?

They seem to have everything.

Why would they commit such an act?

As you read our story, you will realize that no matter what we did and no matter how hard we tried, we could not find Eric the help he needed. We are not doctors or trained professionals, we are simply a family who wanted desperately to help Eric but in failing to do so, we lost one of the greatest gifts God ever gave us.

CHAPTER 1

A FATHER AND MOTHER REMEMBER

The Early Years

The greatest gifts God gave us were our children. The greatest task He put before us was to raise those children. The greatest pain He helped us endure was when we lost a child.

Only someone who has lost a child can understand the pain I am speaking of. This pain consumes you and never goes away. When you lose your child, you lose a part of yourself and you will never be the same. People may look at you and think you are doing well. At times, you can still laugh and carry on a normal conversation. But ultimately, you are not well and are forever changed.

xxxxx

After twelve hours of hard labor, a breech birth with forceps, just after one in the afternoon on December 2, 1968, our son finally came into this world. He weighed 7 lbs 7 ounces, and was 21" long. He had no hair, red marks on his face, and a pointed head caused by the forceps. Not the prettiest baby, some might have thought. But to his father and to me, he was breath-takingly beautiful. I was in the hospital for five days and finally on the fifth day, we agreed on a name. I chose Eric and Bob picked his middle name Gabriel.

"After the angel?" I asked.

"No, after Roman Gabriel the football player," he replied.

I spelled it with an extra "e" on the birth certificate to make him special and different from others with the same name, so we finally had our *Eric Gaberiel Varner.*

It was a challenge at first. Eric had colic and cried a lot for the first few months but otherwise he was a healthy baby crawling early and walking at nine months. As a toddler, he often had nose bleeds but the doctor gave him a vitamin K shot (for clotting) and that took care of the problem.

We lived in Davenport, Iowa when Eric was born and I was a stay-at-home mom.

Having seldom been out of Unionville, Missouri (the small town where I grew up) Davenport was a huge city to me, way bigger than anywhere I had ever been and I was totally in awe of my new surroundings. It didn't take me long to decide that I could either sit at home and be totally dependent on Bob to take me everywhere or I could learn the layout of the town and how to drive in city traffic—so I did the latter. This gave Eric and me the freedom to come and go as we wanted.

We bought a mobile home. The trailer park we were in had three quarter acre lots and was in the country but not far from the hustle and bustle of the city of Davenport.

One day when Bob got home from work he said to Eric, "I have a surprise for you."

"What is it? " Eric asked him in excitement, but then he saw it: a white German Shepherd puppy!

To say he was thrilled would be an understatement. Right away, we knew they were going to have a very special bond. Eric named the puppy Pax, after a white German Shepherd that was on a TV show at that time. Eric was four when Pax joined our family. Eric and Pax were the best of friends and were inseparable; you never saw one without the other.

One day, Bob asked me "Have you seen Eric? I've looked and looked and cannot find him anywhere. He and Pax were outside playing but I can't find Pax either, where are they?"

I heard the concern in Bob's voice and I could tell he was becoming more worried by the minute. I joined in the hunt. For almost a half hour, we looked and we yelled for both of them, but they were nowhere to be found. We went over every place that we had already been over at least ten times. Finally, when we were at our wit's end and scared to death, Bob saw it: a little white wagging tail sticking out from under a tarp that was in the backyard.

Eric knew by the sound of our voices that we were scared and upset. The more we yelled, the more scared and upset we became, so Eric thought it might be best for him and Pax to stay hidden for a little while longer. He knew they were both in big trouble and he was right! His partner in crime was right by his side the whole time and he never barked or whined once.

xxxxx

Eric developed a love for sports at a very young age and he was seldom seen without a ball in his hand. He loved playing baseball with his plastic ball and bat, playing football with a little football just his size, and basketball with a hoop that fit over the top of a door. He was very competitive and especially liked playing any and all sports with his dad.

After five years we had another son, Chad, and two years later we had a daughter, Natalie. We had moved back to our

hometown of Unionville, Missouri by this time and this is where Eric and his siblings grew up and attended school. Bob's family had a farm in the west end of the county and when Bob's father passed away, he wanted to be close to help his mother with the day-to-day operation of the farm.

Unionville is a small town in Northern Missouri about 7 miles from the Iowa state line. It is located in Putnam County. Agriculture is its main resource. Wildlife is plentiful, and hunters come from far away to test their skill at turkey and deer hunting. It was where we grew up and now it was where our children would grow up. While Davenport gave us the convenience of city living, Putnam County gave us the serene country living that one only reads about.

We bought an old farmhouse with 40 acres and we and the previous owners agreed they could keep their horse on the 40 acres until they could find a place to put him. By this time, Eric was seven, Chad was two, and Natalie was just an infant. I had accidentally fallen asleep in the chair only to be awakened by Eric telling me "I fell off the horse and was knocked out."

I saw he had on his cowboy hat and boots as well as a nice bump on his head.

"Why were you on the horse?" I asked him.

"I wanted to ride him," he said.

By this time, he seemed okay so I didn't think I needed to take him to the doctor but I later learned that he more than likely had a concussion. This would be the first of many more concussions to come. We eventually sold the old house and forty acres and built a new house just up the road.

Even though we were living in the country, Eric was lucky enough to have boys his age as close neighbors. They would all gather at our house for a game of one-on-one basketball that would last until dark. When it got so dark they couldn't see they would continue to play under the security light that was in our driveway with Bob and Chad sometimes joining in. There were times we would have to make them quit playing because it was getting late and there was school the next day. When they weren't playing basketball they were engaged in a game of football.

Eric started school at a small country school for grades K-8. After that, the students all went to a larger school known as Putnam County R-I, located in Unionville, to finish grades 9-12. While attending the school in the country, he had to ride the school bus. He was the first one on at 7:20 A.M. and the last one off at 4:30 P.M.

I remember how I hated going to parent-teacher conferences. Bob was always busy with work, so I went by myself. I heard the same thing from his teachers year after year: "Eric plays too rough with the other kids, he doesn't apply himself, and he does not work to his potential." One of his teachers even told me "Eric only got a C in Math." Frankly, I thought a C wasn't all that bad considering it was Math, a subject that Eric had always found difficult.

When I first heard the teachers describe Eric, it upset me and I would tell Bob about the conference, and we would discuss their comments with Eric. We eventually came to terms with it and we decided that what they said really wasn't that bad nor did it matter. We knew our son and even though he played too rough and didn't always work up to his potential (and got a C in Math) we knew he would do just fine in life—we were sure of it.

After the eighth grade, Eric started going to the larger school in Unionville. By this time, the two schools had consolidated and Chad and Natalie went there as well. I worked in Unionville, so I could drop them off as I went to work which meant no more early bus rides. Eric adapted well to the larger school, as did his brother and sister, and I did not dread parent-teacher's conferences as I once had.

Recently, I ran into one of Eric's friends. He told me that he thinks of Eric often and he has so many good memories of them when they were growing up. He said that when they were in elementary school, he would often come home mad and upset and he would tell his mother.

"We had a race today and I came in second again! I am so mad! I am always second and Eric is always first. My mother would work with me and we would try to develop a plan that would guarantee me a first place finish—it never worked. Eric was always first no matter how good our plan was."

We both laughed and I told him that I was sure he had many athletic abilities that Eric didn't have. He was one of the neighbor boys that often played basketball and football at our house and by the time he and Eric were in high school, they were the starting players for their school's football team.

I remember one night when Eric was 13 and we were all asleep. Eric woke us up crying and holding his ear. Eric never cried no matter how hurt or how much pain he was in, so we knew this was bad.

Nothing we could do would help him, so I told Bob that I would take him to the emergency room, calling in advance to let them know we are coming. Eric and I headed to the hospital while Bob stayed home with Chad and Natalie. When Eric and I got back home, I told Bob about the look on the faces of the nurses at the registration desk when they saw Eric standing there, taller than me by this time. One of them said, "Oh, wow, we thought you were bringing in a little boy — we didn't realize he was this big!" This would have been funny had it not been for Eric feeling so awful. Eric, like his father, had allergies and they had been especially bad during this time, causing him to blow his nose so hard that he had burst his eardrum. I don't know what the doctor did, but by the time we had left the hospital Eric was feeling better and was able to rest once we got back home.

When your child hurts or is in pain, you hurt and you feel the pain with them. We couldn't have known then, but the pain we would feel with Eric later in his life would be much worse then the burst eardrum we had just experienced.

SPORTS

Soon the coaches began to notice Eric's athletic ability and by the time he was a sophomore, he was one of the players you threw the ball to if you wanted a touchdown. The fact that he "played rough" was now an asset.

On Wednesday, before the football game on Friday, Bob would start getting nervous and he would have butterflies just thinking about Friday's game. It was accurate to say that he was way more nervous than Eric. Eric played in pain most of the time due primarily to a foot injury that he had gotten early on; but he never complained, he just toughed it out. The injury didn't heal the way it should have and when he walked you heard a "popping" sound. This continued for the rest of his life.

The best football game Eric had during his high school years was against Putnam County's biggest rival. He had a total of 284 yards running and receiving even though he sat out most of the fourth quarter. The game was on film and he managed to get a copy of it and he and his dad would watch it over and over discussing it play by play. The competitive nature he had as a child was now quite prominent. Eric loved performing for his coaches and the crowd and no injury or pain was going to keep him from playing his best.

Eric came home with his fingers bandaged one day.

"What happened to your hand?" I asked.

"I hurt it in practice so the coach took me to the hospital to have it X-Rayed and two of my fingers are broke."

"Why didn't they call and let me and your Dad know before they made the decision to take you to the doctor?"

Eric shrugged and that was the end of the conversation with him. I told Bob about it but it wasn't a big deal to him either. I appeared to be the only one that didn't like the fact someone else was taking charge of our son's medical treatment without talking to us first. Once again, I realized how important football was to Eric and his father. They would often tell me that "You don't understand — you don't understand the game of football!" They were right, I didn't understand and I did not care to find out.

I remember going to one of Eric's football games that was out of town. The bleachers were only on one side of the field which meant the home team spectators and the visitors had to sit together. I ended up sitting next to a woman from the opposing team. She was quite loud and very obnoxious and I was uncomfortable with the comments she was yelling at the football players, mostly aimed at our team's boys. I finally realized that when she yelled "Kill him! Kill him! Break his legs!" it was meant for Eric. I wanted so badly to say something to the woman but as angry as she seemed to be, I was sure my words would only provoke her. I could not understand how, I presumed she was a mother of one of the players, she could feel so strongly about a football game and be so mean spirited.

Eric never gave us much trouble or reason to worry. He was usually very responsible and trustworthy. Except once, it was late, way past his curfew, and his father and I were up pacing and watching the clock. We made calls to all of his friends with whom we thought he might be with and all were home except for one. So, we presumed that was who he was with. It got to be later and needless to say, we were worried sick. We just knew he had been in a car wreck and was dead lying in a ditch somewhere. I remember thinking to myself that we would have to bury him in his letter jacket because it was that important to him. What a morbid thought for a mother to have! I had a sick feeling in my stomach. Once again, little did I know it would be something we would have to face years later.

Bob was getting ready to go to look for him when he finally pulled in the drive. We didn't know whether to be mad or glad, I guess both. Needless to say he was grounded for a month. This was the only time he ever did anything disrespectful or irresponsible. We were so relieved that he was home safe that we didn't ask him where he had been. He never volunteered the information and to this day, we still don't know why he was so late. I suppose some things are best left alone. He was safe — that's all we cared about!

As Eric went from year to year through high school, he became better and better in sports. Not only in football but in track and field as well.

He set records in six different track events; his royal blue and white letter jacket (the school colors) was weighed down with over a hundred medals plus honor patches that he earned in football, track and field, and basketball. His classmates joked that they knew when he was coming down the hall because they could hear the medals on his letter jacket jingling. College coaches began looking at him and his senior year he was recruited and got a scholarship to play football and run track at Graceland College in Lamoni, Iowa. He received many honors and awards at the college level as well.

As time went on, the weight from all of the medals wore out the letter jacket and after he married his wife, they had the medals and patches put in a framed display for everyone to see.

COLLEGE YEARS

When Eric left for college, we missed him terribly. Along with football and track practice, classes, and working, he seldom made it home. But when he did, it was only for a short time. I don't think Eric ever missed home that much, he had always been independent and seldom asked us for anything, unless it was maybe some money from time to time.

I remember going to visit him and since it was his first year of college, he was required to live on campus. The dorm room was small and the walls were a dingy color. There was only one window to let in the outside light.

As was, and is still quite common, Eric did not know his roommate but he was the type that could get along with anyone and everyone. We knew without asking which side of the dorm room was Eric's. One side of the room had a poster of Farrah Fawcett and a poster of the rock group, KISS. The other side had posters of airplanes and fighter jets....it was obvious which side was Eric's (it wasn't the side with the airplanes and fighter jets). We had to admit the posters helped to bring some color and life to the room though.

We were lucky enough to be able to attend almost all of Eric's college football games. I distinctly remember one where he went up to catch a pass and was sandwiched between two players from the opposing team, knocking him out.

I said to his Dad, "Doesn't anyone care that our son is lying out cold on the field? All they care about is that he caught the ball!"

Bob was heading to the field to check on him when he finally came to his senses. He went out of the game only to return a short time later. Another concussion to add to the ones he had previously gotten. Back then however, if someone received a hit on the head that resulted in a concussion, it wasn't a big deal. Only much later did we learn that head trauma would prove to be way more serious than anyone knew at the time.

Because it was his first year in college, his college sent us a copy of his grades. We noticed there were several Ws on the grade report and I asked him,

"Do the Ws mean that you are weak in these classes?"

He just laughed and said, "No, that means I withdrew from those classes."

Bob and I weren't sure if that was a good thing or bad thing, but he graduated with a degree in Health and Physical Education, so he apparently knew what he was doing!

His second year of college, he lived off campus with some of his friends but still within walking distance of the college. If we were upset about the dorm room, the house he was in now was no comparison. It was far, far, worse.

"Oh my!" were the only words I could say when I saw it.

Bob replied "'Oh my' is right!"

It was an old, old two story house. The floors were uneven, covered with old dirty carpet and creaked when you walked on them. The kitchen appliances were old and probably hadn't been cleaned for quite some time from the looks of them and we were pretty sure there was little to no insulation. To make things worse, his room was on the top floor.

We didn't want to act too shocked when we saw Eric, so we chose our words carefully. We did not want him to think we were being critical.

"You might want to put an escape plan in place just in case of fire or carbon monoxide poisoning. Such a plan is always good to have no matter where you live."

His father reiterated how important such a plan would be. What we didn't say was that we were sure this house could not possibly survive another year of college boys and we feared the worst.

However, the house miraculously remained standing through the rest of his college years. After that, Bob talked him in to coming home until he could find a job that his college education had prepared him for.

MARRIED LIFE

Eric dispatched at the local sheriff's office where he had worked part time while in high school. It wasn't long until he got a job with the Missouri Department of Public Safety as a liquor control agent. The job required him to move an hour and half away to Chillicothe, Missouri, a town twice the size of Unionville, and this is where he met his wife.

Her name was Sara and she was a teacher in the local school system. Sara was tall and thin with long dark hair and brown eyes. She was as beautiful as he was handsome, so they made the perfect couple. All of their family and friends knew that this was "the one" for both of them.

After dating for some time, they decided to get married. The wedding was held at Sandals Resort in Jamaica. We were not there, but they gave us a video of the ceremony that was held outside. The happy couple was surrounded by white sandy beaches, crystal blue water, and a cloudless powder blue sky—it was picture-perfect. Eric looked so handsome and Sara looked so beautiful; they could have been on the cover of a magazine. Unfortunately however, the picture-perfect couple would not stay perfect forever.

THE MOVE

While living in Chillicothe, they had a son, Brett, and eighteen months later, a daughter, Lauryn. After about five years working as a liquor control agent, Eric got a job with a medical supply company and a short time later he got a job as a pharmaceutical sales representative; this job would require the family to move to Cape Girardeau, Missouri.

Cape Girardeau, or "Cape" as the locals call it, is a lovely town in the idyllic setting of the Missouri mountains in the southern part of the state. It is approximately 116 miles south of St. Louis. From Unionville, it takes about seven hours going the scenic way, and six hours if going by interstate. When we would go to visit Eric and his family, both Bob and I preferred the scenic route where you can stop and shop at a number of little tourist towns along the way. "Cape" offered Eric and his family good schools, good health care, and more opportunities for the whole family.

Getting tired of school politics, Sara became a pharmaceutical sales representative as well. So for a while, they were in the same profession. Life was good, they had good jobs, a nice home, they were a church-going family with two beautiful children. Theirs was the perfect life, the perfect family, but then something went terribly wrong.

Living so far away, we were not aware of what was happening in their lives. Being a private person, Eric did not tell us anything other than what he chose to make us believe everything was fine.

I remember Eric came to his brother's wedding but Sara and the children did not come. I asked Eric why and he told me "They had plans to go out of town with her family." I thought this was strange and that there was probably more to the story, but he didn't elaborate and I did not ask anything further.

He was terribly thin, having lost a lot of weight from the last time we had seen him. When I mentioned this to him, he said, "I have been trying to lose weight and I have been on a diet."

A mother's intuition is a powerful thing. I told Bob that I was afraid there was something wrong with Eric. As most men would do, he told me, "I am sure you are making too much of nothing and that everything is fine."

Eric had a lot of injuries from years of playing football and was in pain most of his adult life. We later learned that he had been addicted to painkillers. He told us that kicking the addiction was one of the hardest things he had ever done.

It was about this time Eric began to change. He quit his job, explaining that he wanted to be home more and that he would find another job that didn't require him to be gone so much. Unfortunately, this was at a time when the unemployment rate was high and jobs were not as plentiful as they once were—at least not the kind of job to which he was accustomed.

HEALTH CONCERNS

Eric became jealous and was convinced his wife was seeing someone else. He had phone numbers of individuals whom he believed she was involved with. Knowing Sara like we did and how much she loved her family, we seriously doubted the accuracy of what Eric was telling us.

Sara called us one evening and was very upset. She told us that Eric was not well and she told us about how he was acting and some of the things he was doing. Paranoid thoughts such as thinking there were cameras and bugging devices in their home. At that time, we did not know of Eric's paranoia and all we knew was what he was telling us. So in turn, we dismissed what Sara was saying. We later learned that was a mistake and we should have listened to her. Our suspicions that he wasn't well were becoming all too true.

Eric went to doctors and they gave him tests, put him on medication for depression, schizophrenia, and bipolar disorder. Eric and Sara managed to stay together for another two years, in attempts to hold the family together, but they ended up getting a divorce in 2010.

DARK DAYS AHEAD

Seeing that he was not getting any better, his brother Chad went to see him and convinced him to come home. After all, we were sure the love of a mother and father could fix whatever problems he was having and we wanted him close. We did not realize the extent of his paranoia and health problems until he got home. Eric told us things we knew could not possibly be true and what we were hearing only convinced us more, that he needed help.

Eric told us about events that had taken place, such as the time he was crossing the bridge from Illinois into Missouri. Eric told us that he got a call from a friend telling him that he needed to be careful crossing the bridge because there were people in orange shirts following him; then the military arrived, and the people in the orange shirts disappeared. When he got across the bridge there was someone there taking his picture. On another occasion, he said he was at his daughter's ball game and there was a big guy sitting behind his wife. He started doing hand signals to other individuals in the crowd.

There were many stories similar to these. He would become very agitated when telling us about them. At the end of each story he would say, "I want answers why this happened!" As crazy as they were to us, Eric totally believed they had happened.

Eric also told us there were bugging devices in their home and in his car. Being several hundred miles away, we did not know what was taking place but the more we talked with him, we realized something was not right. We called and talked to a good friend of his who lived in Cape Girardeau who had also heard these same stories and he assured us that the stories Eric told us had never happened.

Only to convince us more that he needed to be close, was when we found out that he had been found unconscious on the sidewalk in downtown Cape. He had been beaten up and just left there. We tried hard to get a copy of the police report but never received one. We presumed that he accused someone of doing something they had not done and they retaliated by beating him up.

When Eric got back to Unionville, he stayed with us for a short time until Chad found him a house close to where he lived. It wasn't long before he left there and moved into a house at Lake Thunderhead. Lake Thunderhead is a recreational lake three miles North of Unionville. The lake offers many things to do such as boating, swimming, golfing, and tennis; all things Brett and Lauryn would enjoy when they would come for a visit. The house was on a waterfront lot and was very nice and spacious—plenty of room for company.

Eric got a job at a nearby television station in their sales department but you could tell he was like a time bomb waiting to explode. Bob knew how to talk to him better than me. I was always afraid I would say the wrong thing that would send him over the edge, so I avoided anything that might upset him. All while trying to let him know how much we all loved him and that we wanted to help.

Eric and his dad spent time together. Bob made sure things got taken care of at this house and that he had everything he needed. All I knew to offer was plenty to eat. Occasionally his sister, Natalie and I would clean his house and wash his clothes; but no matter what we did, nothing was helping.

A friend of his from college came to visit Eric and ended up at our house because he was concerned by Eric's actions and feared he might try and hurt himself. Eric was acting crazy, waving a gun around and saying things that made no sense and threatening to kill himself. We called the sheriff and he went with us to Eric's house. That night, we took him to an emergency room but they did nothing for him and couldn't even tell us what to do. After Eric was put in a room, he asked Natalie: "There is something wrong with me, isn't there?" Natalie replied, "Yes."

The lack of attention from medical facilities would become all too familiar. Since Eric wasn't getting any better, we did a court-ordered 96 hour hold that allowed us to admit him to a medical facility (without his consent) that could treat his problems. This was the hardest thing we ever had to do, but if we wanted to help Eric, we had to do whatever was necessary. We went to the Circuit Clerk's Office and completed the required paperwork. Normally in these situations, the court will send the person needing help to one of the state facilities. We were afraid Eric would not get the proper care since the state treatment centers are usually overcrowded and patients seldom get the one-on-one counseling needed to help them. We asked the judge if we could have Eric admitted to a reputable hospital in Columbia, Missouri. Columbia is about three hours from Unionville. It hosts nationally reputable doctors and hospitals. We had firsthand knowledge about the healthcare there because of family and friends who went there for serious health problems. The judge agreed to our request.

On the day Eric had a doctor's visit in Kirksville, Missouri, about 45 minutes from Unionville, the sheriff was there waiting on Eric when he was done with his appointment. He took Eric to the hospital in Columbia while we followed them in our car. We didn't realize that a

96 hour hold did not necessarily mean 96 hours. Eric soon called us and told us, "You can come and get me, they are letting me out. I know how to play this game, I have been through this before!"

Bob was furious and called the hospital to try and find out why they didn't keep him. "Why are you letting Eric come home? Can't you see how badly he needs help?"

The hospital staff thought Bob was threatening them so, in turn, they were not helpful and gave us no answers.

We couldn't believe our ears—they were letting Eric come home in this condition! We thought: *finally, he is in a place that can evaluate him and hopefully help him* but in less than 24 hours, they were sending him home—with no answers!

As we pulled up to the hospital entrance to pick Eric up, a young doctor, who had been part of Eric's medical team came running out to the car before Eric got there and handed Bob a prescription. "Make sure Eric takes this medication, I can't discuss with you what is wrong with him but it is important he takes the medication as prescribed."

DARKER DAYS COMING

One morning, Eric stopped by our house to get his medications that we had picked up for him. You could always tell he was not having a good day by his body language and how he responded to our questions. We should have realized it was a "Bad Eric" day and did not question him about anything but we asked if he was taking the medication the way in which the instructions said. This was too much and it sent him into a rage. He was yelling at us: "If you want to help me, find out why people are following me, and why there are bugging devices in my car!" He gave us 73 pages of phone numbers and license plate numbers that he had written down (an example of his erratic behavior) and he wanted us to find out to whom they belonged.

"This is what you can do if you want to help me!"

I had listened to his ranting. All I could do (I am ashamed to say) was to yell and cry, to make him understand that all we were doing was helping him. I was trying to convey that all of these numbers were not the problem, that he needed medical help. Poor Bob (the only one of the three of us that stayed cool and calm) now had two of us with whom he was dealing. But with some much-needed reasoning, he managed to get us both under control. Needless to say, to help defuse the situation we took the 70+ pages of numbers and told Eric we would try to find out what we could about them.

Witnessing more than once that Eric had a short fuse and angered easily, we realized that he was not the same person he used to be and that his personality had totally changed.

A friend of his told us about the time they were in line at a convenience store and Eric started an altercation with the people behind him, accusing them of following him. And another time at a ball game the same thing happened, but his friend stopped it before an all-out fight started.

Eric often complained of headaches, he had trouble sleeping, and his blood pressure was always high, despite the medication he took for it. His beautiful blue eyes were not the same, he was always rolling and rubbing them; his eyes told us there was something terribly, terribly wrong.

Our three kids were not close when they were growing up, but suddenly there was a powerful bond between them. We were fortunate to have both Chad, now 39 and Natalie, 37, living close. Chad, his wife, and their daughter, lived about ten miles west of Unionville. Natalie, her husband, and their three sons lived just a mile outside of Unionville. Eric, Chad, and Natalie spent a lot of time together. Chad and Natalie tried as hard as we did to help Eric, but all of our efforts were in vain; whatever was going on with him was very powerful and we couldn't conquer it.

In December of 2011, he became very ill and had to have surgery for a twisted colon. He became more depressed and ended up quitting his job (or was fired; we were never sure what happened) in January of 2012. Eric missed his children and with them so far away, he didn't get to see them as much as he would have liked.

CHAPTER 2

MARCH 22, 2012

Bob and I would call to check on Eric daily, just to make sure he was okay and to see if he needed anything. On Thursday, March 22, 2012, one day before his dad's birthday, he did not answer any of our calls; his phone went straight to voicemail. I remember getting home from work around 4:30 P.M. and asking Bob: "Have you talked with Eric today? I have tried several times to call him but never got an answer."

Bob said he had called as well and had not talked with him either. At this point, we became uneasy. I called Natalie to find out what she knew and if she had talked with Eric. I called her home phone and her husband, Jamie, answered. I could tell right away something was wrong. He told me, "I just got a call from Natalie and she was crying and screaming, I couldn't understand her; I am getting ready to go to Eric's house."

I immediately called Natalie on her cell phone and she answered crying; she was so upset that I couldn't understand what she was saying.

"Is Eric alright?" I asked, but there was no need for a response. I already knew the answer. It was on this date, March 22, 2012, we lost our son to a self-inflicted gunshot.

We went to his house. We wanted to comfort Natalie and to be alone with Eric for a few minutes before the funeral home came to take him away. Bob and I sat with him, we took his hands in ours; I put my face in his hand and I saw the little boy playing with his beloved dog, Pax. I saw the little boy that would ride his Big Wheel down the steep hill by our house, but waited for us to push it back up. The same little boy who made his mother the most wonderful cookbook (I still have it) when he was in kindergarten.

Then someone, we don't remember who, jolted us back to reality and told us that the coroner was on the way and that it might be best if we would leave him now. Our legs were like rubber, but somehow they managed to carry us outside where we collapsed on the ground.

We saw the hearse pull in and the coroner, sheriff, and some other people went inside with a gurney. It wasn't long until they came out with a black bag on the gurney and we knew; we knew that our son was in that horrible black bag. I looked at Bob and he was looking down; it was as if he couldn't make himself look at the scene that was playing out before us. I wanted to scream at the top of my lungs: "NO, NO, BRING HIM BACK, THIS IS ALL A MISTAKE, THIS CAN'T BE!"

And I asked myself:

Why didn't I wrap my arms around him and hold him when we were inside—Why? Why?

I knew without Bob saying a word that he was thinking the same thing, It was at that moment, we both realized that we would never again hold our son.

We will never forget that day: March 22, 2012. The memory of it will always be with us. We just wanted it to be a bad dream, one that we would wake up from. This couldn't be reality; it couldn't be our son that they were taking away. But it was and it was real.

DEATH OF A CHILD

In a small town, word travels quickly. It seemed like it was just minutes before people started coming by the house, most to bring food and others to pay their respect. Bob and I stayed in the family room at the back of the house. My sisters and nieces kept people from us, knowing that we needed to be alone. They greeted visitors and thanked them for the food or for just coming by, but they knew we were in no shape to talk with anyone. We couldn't think straight; we had just lost our son, our child. How do you talk to anyone when you are that consumed with pain?

There were funeral arrangements to be made and matters to be taken care of. We had to get a grip at least long enough to get these things done. We asked about Brett and Lauryn and if anyone had called their mother. We were told Chad had called her. We felt bad; we couldn't even think about how they must be feeling or about their pain, we were so consumed with our own pain.

When I did think about his family, I was mad. *How could he have done such a thing to all of us? How could he leave those two wonderful, beautiful children without a father—what was he thinking?*

That was the problem. He wasn't thinking, at least not rationally. I am sure that in his mind, he thought he was doing us all a favor.

We went to the funeral home and made the arrangements. I remember we picked out the casket, wrote the obituary, and told the funeral director what song we wanted to have played. I picked the song, "How Great Thou Art (My Chains Are Gone)." It is a song we often sing in church and it's one of our favorites. We were planning a funeral for our child, we were picking out a casket for our child. This is not the normal way life is to go; a parent should never outlive their children.

The day of the service was a beautiful spring day. The whole week was sunny and warm. Bob and I both said how glad we were that it was not rainy or cold. In Missouri, March weather can be unpredictable. If there was anything to be thankful for on our darkest day, it was that it was sunny outside.

As always, it was his siblings, Chad and Natalie, who saw that things were taken care of on the day of the service. There were pictures of Eric and his children in happy times alongside his football jersey, sports awards, work accolades, and other items that gave everyone a glimpse of his life and the kind of person he was—it was a beautiful tribute to him.

Visitation was an hour before the service. All I can remember was that I was like a robot. I would hug the person coming past me and thank them for coming. Hug and "Thank you for coming." Hug and "Thank you for coming." This was all I had to offer, this was the best I could do. I was so worried about Bob having a hard time, I didn't know if he would make it through this part of the service. But somehow, by the grace of God, we all survived it.

The funeral was nice. There were many flowers and a lot of people came to pay their respects. High school classmates, college friends, and former co-workers were all there, many coming from far distances. They were there because they wanted to be and because it was important to them to be there for Eric.

Eric belonged to a Methodist Church in Cape Girardeau, but since that was so far away we asked the senior minister at the Christian Church to which we belong to conduct the service. His best friend from college spoke, then Chad came to us and asked, "Do either of you care if I say a few words?"

We nodded our approval and I remember thinking to myself, *Oh my gosh, what in the world is he going to say?* Bob made no comment and I wondered if he was thinking the same thing. Our fears were unfounded because he did a great job. Unfortunately, neither of us can remember what he said, but then again, we don't remember a lot about that day.

LIFE WITHOUT ERIC

For a while, Bob went to the cemetery every day. He sowed grass seed, watered and pulled weeds around the tombstone. I went with him because I felt that he needed me to be there with him. But it soon became very hard for me to do. While some people find comfort in visiting the grave of their loved one, I do not. I would look at the stone with Eric's picture and name on it and it was like a knife would go through my heart. I knew he was gone, but being there and seeing it was a tragic reminder of that painful day and I finally quit going. Bob was never upset about my not going. I never told him why I didn't want to go, but I believe he knew why I felt the way I did and understood. I have (with time) gotten better. I can now sometimes go with him to visit the grave and to help decorate it. It hasn't gotten any less painful. I am convinced that it never will.

DARKNESS

When we lost Eric, the pain was unbearable, as it would have been if it had been Chad or Natalie. I was so consumed with the pain, that my mind was telling me to give up and to slip into a dark place. That place that makes you not want to get up in the morning, that makes you want to sleep all day so you don't have to think and you don't have to feel. In that place, you are not in reality, you hear and see those around you but your mind goes in a hundred different directions and you can't concentrate or focus on anyone or anything but pain. After a while, it becomes your comfort zone because it's the place where you like being and the place where the pain and depression have become your best friend. In that place, you don't care about anyone else or how they are feeling; you are like a zombie—existing, but yet not existing at all. You don't care if you live or die because if you die, then you will get to be with the one you lost. The word "death" has become your entire vocabulary and you worry if someone else you love will die suddenly.

I recall seeing young children and I wondered if they would grow up to commit suicide. I remembered Eric when he was little and how he too was a normal, happy child and I prayed that those children's parents never had to experience such a loss. While my mind was telling me one thing, my heart and my faith were telling me to keep going, to be strong, and that somehow we would all survive this.

Soon, Bob was escaping to the quiet of the country. To the place where he hunts, where it is quiet, and where he could be alone and deal with his emotions in private. I was doing the opposite. I wanted to hear the sound of cars coming and going, to see the neighbors outside in their yards and to hear the faint voices and the familiar faces of those on their morning walk as they went past our house. They were so absorbed in their conversation with one another they had no idea anyone was paying any attention to them. They had no idea someone found them therapeutic. I needed to know there was still life around me and I wanted to know that some people were able to carry on their normal routine and that nothing had changed for them. They had not lost a child, so they had no idea of the pain my family and I were feeling. I was glad for them but at the same time I wondered if we would (or if we could) ever be normal again.

I started writing this book soon after Eric died because it helped me deal with the feelings and emotions that I wasn't comfortable talking about to anyone. Bob, Chad, and Natalie were dealing with their own pain and I didn't want to be an added burden to the emotional load they were already carrying.

TV was my escape. When I would say it aloud, it sounded so crazy and I am sure if anyone heard me say it they thought so too. However, they were not in my shoes and would not understand how, for just a few minutes, my mind was occupied by something other than my thoughts. It was like a breath of fresh air for mere moments, but it was soon gone. Whatever I was watching took second place to the realization of how our lives had changed and how they would never be the same again for any of us.

CHAPTER 3

CHAD'S STORY
Brotherly Love

Being Eric Varner's little brother had its upside and its downside. If you didn't know we were brothers, you probably would have never guessed it. The only thing that we had in common were our blue eyes—what some people referred to as "The Varner Eyes". My Dad has those blue eyes and my mother's are brown. Eric, Natalie, and I inherited Dad's blue eyes but other than that, we were totally different.

As far back as I can remember, Eric was always full of confidence and determination; whatever he wanted, he got it. Most importantly, he believed in himself—a trait I often envied.

Being five years younger and half his size, I had little going for me when it came to not doing what he told me to do or in fighting back. Like the time he threw me in the dryer and turned it on then stood in front of the door so I couldn't open it! Luckily, he did think enough of me to let me out before I died. Something for which I am eternally grateful. I remember he would ask me to shoot baskets with him, but I came to the conclusion the only reason he wanted me to play was so he could have a good reason to pound me in the ground. Also, he wanted to show off his talent, since I never made a basket and he made every shot. Sometimes Dad would join in the fun, so I was now playing with two giants (at least that is how it seemed at the time). Being half their size made it virtually impossible for me to throw the ball over or around them to shoot—I couldn't even see over or around them! At least Eric didn't pound me to the ground when Dad played with us.

"Stay out of my car!" was Eric's favorite saying to me. He was super particular about his cars and I was not to get in them, or to even touch them because he knew I would get them dirty (he was probably right). I was never as particular or clean as he was—another example of how we differed.

If there was a mud hole, I went through it and Eric went around it. He was particular about his dress and appearance and I would just throw something on—sometimes digging it out of the dirty clothes while trying not to let Mom catch me doing so.

Eric's first car was a 1977 two-toned gold Oldsmobile Cutlass. It was a nice car and was passed down to me when he was done with it. His next car was a red 1978 Pontiac Trans Am. It looked good on the outside but it was a real dud. There was always something wrong and it was in the repair shop more than it was out. I couldn't help but think to myself that he probably wished that he had kept the Olds Cutlass!

I loved the country and everything that went with it: hunting, fishing, mudding, everything that went with the outdoors I wanted to do. Eric on the other hand, it wasn't his thing. I seldom remember him ever going hunting or fishing with me and Dad.

I do remember one time he said to me, "I think I will go turkey hunting."

"By yourself?" I asked,

"Why not?" he replied.

Of course, he wouldn't have thought about asking me to go with him. Maybe because he was afraid I was a better shot. Maybe I'd show him up or I might accidentally shoot him—only in the leg of course—because of all the mean things he had done to me over the years. When he got back I asked him "Where is the turkey? Did you get one?"

"I didn't see any turkeys but I shot a coyote."

"Where is it?" I asked.

"I left it in the field," he said.

I highly doubted the story that I was hearing. I was pretty certain there was no coyote or turkey; whether it was because he didn't see anything or because he missed them both, I don't know because he never confessed to either scenario. I must admit though that my inner self felt a little vindicated. I even rejoiced a little in the fact that maybe he had actually failed at something and that maybe—just maybe—there was something I was better at than him, even if it was just hunting.

I had a little dirt bike that I loved to ride. One day, Eric jumped on it and took off only to end up crashing into the ditch across the road. Here he came back, limping and carrying the bike and all he could say was: "Don't tell Dad."

I wasn't sure if I wasn't to tell Dad because he tore up my bike, or because he hurt his leg and it might jeopardize how he played in the next football game. Nevertheless, I kept the secret and never told Dad.

When the opportunity would arise and Eric wasn't looking, I would try on his letter jacket. It was so heavy from all the medals on it, for honors he had received in football, basketball, and track, that I could hardly stand up in it. And for just a few minutes, the royal blue and white letter jacket and I became one…but not for long because off it would come in a hurry when I heard Eric coming.

His athletic ability was something I envied and tried my best to emulate but never could. I often heard from his coaches, "Are you going to be as good as your big brother? We can't wait to see what you can do!"

I should have viewed these words as encouragement for me to work hard but unfortunately the words had the opposite effect; I felt defeated without even trying.

As the years went on, Eric became nicer to me. I'm not sure if it was because he liked me better or if he just decided being nice didn't take as much energy as being mean to me; regardless of his reason, I was more than grateful for the change.

When he left for college, we all missed him. Even I missed him but I wasn't about to admit that to anyone. I remember what it was like going and watching him play college football. Everyone from the coaches, to the players, and of course to his friends, all treated me like I was royalty simply because I was Eric Varner's little brother.

The older we got, the less and less we saw of each other. The only times we were together would occasionally be at family functions, but other than that we seldom talked on the phone or visited one another.

I had been hearing from my sister, Natalie, as well as Mom and Dad, that something was going on with Eric and they feared he wasn't well. My wife and I took it upon ourselves, without telling anyone, to go to Cape Girardeau to see if everyone's fears were warranted or if their imaginations were running wild. He was divorced by this time and living in a small apartment. I could tell from talking with him that everyone was right, something was wrong, but I had no idea what it was.

Eric told us that people were in his apartment, specifically the waiters that worked at a nearby restaurant and that people were on his roof and he could hear them at night. Miraculously, I talked him in to coming back home with us. It was obvious he was at the point that he didn't know what he wanted or where he wanted to go: somewhere, anywhere that could help him with his pain.

On the way home, he told us that people had put cameras in his house and were watching him and he saw helicopters that were not there. You could tell he really believed what he was telling us but you also knew by how crazy the stories were, they had never happened.

I tried to help Eric as much as I could once we got him home. I helped him find a place to live and talked with him on a regular basis. I remember one night we went riding around and he was saying all sorts of crazy things. I didn't correct him for fear of upsetting him but I did call Mom and Dad afterward and told them that he really, really needed help.

The day Eric killed himself, I don't think anyone could believe it. It was Eric, my brother. The one who used to give me so much grief when we were little. The one who had such charisma. The one I admired so much.

What on Earth happened?

What went wrong?

What did we miss?

I remember going with Mom, Dad, and Natalie to the funeral home and it was like an out-of-body experience, it didn't seem real. I couldn't wrap my head around the fact Eric had committed suicide and we were planning his funeral.

I tried to hide my pain in hopes of helping everyone else—Mom and Dad, Natalie, and most of all, Brett and Lauryn. But words are just that: words. I don't think there is anything anyone can say at a time like that that will help someone feel better. Besides, I was out of words, I only had questions to which no one had the answers.

During the service, I asked Mom and Dad if they cared if I said a few words. They looked at me as if they had not heard me correctly, but they nodded their approval and I proceeded to the podium. I don't remember what I said, I just knew I could not let this moment pass without telling everyone how special Eric Varner—the son, the father, and the big brother was and how much we would all miss him.

I never saw Eric after he killed himself, even though I was at his house with everyone else after it happened. I never went inside, nor did I view his body at the funeral home. I wanted to remember Eric as he was in life, not in death.

I think about Eric every day, we all miss him terribly. How I would love to play basketball with him again, to question his hunting skills, or to just relive all the mean things he did to me when we were young—if we could just have him back.

When I hear that someone has committed suicide, I feel sympathy for the victim because of the pain they must have felt, but most of all I feel empathy for the family and what they are going through and the pain they are feeling. I know their life will never be the same. Their lives will never be normal again and there will always be something missing. A piece of their heart is now gone. We know this because a piece of our hearts left the day Eric left us.

CHAPTER 4

NATALIE'S STORY
My Big Brother

"I love you, Eric and I miss you every day. I would give anything to hear you laugh again and to see your beautiful blue eyes. I am so honored to be your little sister and I am so glad you are my big brother! Love and miss you every day…"

-Sis

"Oh those blue eyes," or "the jingle, jingle from all the medals on his letter jacket"—those are the words I would hear people say whenever I would mention my big brother's name. And no lie, Eric had the prettiest blue eyes in the whole town or anywhere for that matter. You would know he was coming when you heard the jingle from the medals on his letter jacket representing all the honors he had earned in football, basketball, and track. The jacket is now gone, worn out from the weight of the medals that have been carefully placed in a framed display for us to look at and remember the son, the older brother, the dad and the all-around athlete that my big brother was. I remember when I was young and going to his football games, we always had to leave early enough so Dad could get his seat in the stands on the 50 yard line. I never understood why he always had to sit right in that same place but we all made sure we were ready to go so we could get there before everyone else and Dad could claim "his spot".

Looking out on the field and seeing Eric's iconic #3 was great, but the best thing was hearing, "VARNER FOR THE TOUCHDOWN!" Sitting in the stands with my friends and getting to say, "That's my brother" was amazing!

Not only was he talented in football but watching Eric in track was another experience. I would watch him in the long jump and I don't know if it was because I was young, but when he would jump, it was like I was watching him fly.

It seemed like he was in the air forever. Basketball was the least of the sports that he excelled in and that made it my least favorite to watch. To be honest, I was more interested in watching the cheerleaders and visiting with my friends but I do remember watching him running up and down the court and thinking: *Wow, he really is fast!*

That is what most people remember about my big brother—how amazing he was in sports and that is fine with me, just as long as they always remember him.

We were not close when we were growing up. I was only two years younger than Chad, but seven years younger than Eric and to him, I was the pesky little sister who was always in the way. But we were siblings and it was obvious that we loved each other, even though we did not always show it.

When Eric and his family moved to Cape Girardeau, we saw less and less of him. He had divorced, so Chad went to check on him and to see how he was doing and to everyone's surprise, he convinced Eric to come home.

At first, he stayed with Mom and Dad. I would go check on him and visit with him. I would ask about his children and he would ask about mine. We discussed the weather and whatever else we could think of or I would just sit and look at him and think to myself how handsome he was.

My husband, Jamie, used to tell me he thought Eric was overconfident in school. Eric was a few years older than him, so they never hung out together and were not around each other much until he moved back. Jamie soon realized that he had only known Eric on the outside and after getting to truly know him, he admitted that his early perception of him had been wrong and they soon became good friends.

Eric moved out of Mom and Dad's having found a nice rental house at Lake Thunderhead. The lake had many activities that Brett and Lauryn would enjoy and was not far from town. We spent a lot of time together; he would come over for supper or we would go to his house and order pizza. It was important to me that he had someone here to whom he could talk and with whom to do things. Eric and Jamie enjoyed sharing their high school memories with each other and there were many to tell; most bringing loud bursts of laughter from both of them.

I love a story that Jamie tells about the time when he was at Eric's and it got late, so he decided to spend the night. He slept on the couch in the basement and when he woke the next morning, it took him a little while to realize where he was. About that time, Eric popped around the corner and said, "Morning! Let's go eat!"

It wasn't long until we started noticing strange things that Eric was doing and things he would say, like "there is someone watching me from the house across the lake" or "I know someone has put bugging devices in my car and house. I have put flour on the floor in front of the door so if it is disturbed when I get home, I will know someone has been here."

It was events such as these, along with the stories that he told Mom, Dad, and Chad, that prompted me to say to my parents: "This isn't the brother I know, this is not how he acted three years ago when we attended his 40th surprise birthday party. Something has happened! This is not the same Eric; something isn't right!"

Late one night, I got a call from Chad telling me to "get to Eric's quick, something is wrong." When we got there, Mom and Dad were there, along with a friend of Eric's from college, Chad, and the sheriff. He was fighting with his friend, acting crazy, waving a gun around, doing and saying things that we knew he would never do or say if he was in his right mind. Soon after this, my folks tried a 96 hour hold so he could be assessed at a medical facility and hopefully get some help. The mental health system in Missouri is *terrible*, and he was released EARLY! He was mad at us for a while for having him committed, but he soon got over it.

There is one particular time that I remember being at Eric's house; we had been there for quite some time. It was getting late and I was tired and ready to go home. Looking back now, it really bothers me that we didn't stay. I remember him begging us to spend the night: "Please, please spend the night, I am so lonely. We can watch movies then go and have breakfast in the morning."

I remember the expression on his face when he was asking us to stay and I now wonder if we had, if it would have helped him. I wonder if he was scared since he thought people were following him and us being there would have helped him to sleep. I will never know.

Another time, he was at our house watching TV. I looked at Eric and his eyes were no longer that beautiful blue—they were a dark color, almost black. This bothered me a great deal. We all knew there was something terribly wrong with him and we would all call and check on him daily while trying to find the help he needed. We so badly wanted him to be the Eric we all knew.

Thursday, March 22, 2012: a day that none of us will forget — a day I relive on a lot of nights when I close my eyes. It was a Thursday and it started out beautiful, warm, and sunny. I was at work trying to get things done since I was going to be off for a few days for medical reasons.

I got a call from my mom asking me, "Have you talked to Eric today? Your Dad and I have both tried calling him but neither of us have gotten an answer."

I said, "No I haven't tried but I will."

As soon as I hung up from talking with Mom, I called Eric but there was no answer. I asked a coworker. "Will you please try calling Eric? Maybe he will answer your call since he won't recognize your number."

She tried but did not get an answer either. By the time I got off work, I was frustrated with him that he wasn't answering any of our calls or texts. I called and told Jamie.

"I am going to go and check on Eric just to make sure he is okay, and to tell him to answer his phone when we call."

Jamie wanted to go with me, but I said, "No, I won't be long."

When I got to his house, his car was in the driveway, so I knew he was home and I became more upset knowing he was there but wasn't answering his phone.

I went in through the basement and it was so hot, the heat hit me as soon as I opened the door and I wondered if Eric had turned the furnace on by mistake. As I made my way upstairs, I started getting cold and I thought that Eric must have the air conditioner turned way up and I was puzzled as to why the furnace was on in the basement and the air conditioner was turned on high up stairs. I felt scared because it was so quiet, too quiet. I opened the door to the hallway and yelled: "Eric, are you here?" And that is when I saw him.

I remember kneeling down in front of him, talking to him, and asking him questions. What I was asking him, I have no idea. I only remember bits and pieces. The next thing I knew I was outside, but I don't know how I got there. I was screaming, "Help me, please someone help me!"

I made my way to the neighbors and started banging on their door, "Help me, help me, please help me," but there was no answer. I dialed 911, but the call wouldn't go through. I vaguely remember calling Jamie but he couldn't understand me because I was crying and screaming hysterically. My mother called and asked me what happened and if Eric was alright and I had to tell her, "No Mom, he is dead, he shot himself."

Finally, a big tall man and his wife were with me. The man put his arm around me and said something but I don't remember what; I was just so glad someone was finally with me. I saw Mom and Dad pull in the drive and run to the house, and then I heard my mom scream. I pushed the kind man away and I went running back into the house.

By this time, Jamie and Chad were there and the next thing I knew we were all standing outside again, all in shock, trying to grasp the fact that Eric had just killed himself.

The ride home was a blur. I got in the shower as soon as we got there and I totally broke down. All the emotions, the pain, the shock of finding him all came to the surface and I started crying uncontrollably. There were no words to describe how I felt.

I couldn't get the picture of him out of my head or the sound of my mother's scream—it was haunting me and still does to this day. I didn't sleep at all that night; every time I closed my eyes I relived every minute of the nightmare that was now controlling our lives, and wondered if and when we would wake up from it, yet knowing that we never would. I remember saying, "My big brother committed suicide. He is gone. What are we going to do without him? I never thought he would do such a thing."

Word of what happened was soon all over town and it wasn't long until people started coming by. I remember my cousin being there and both of us crying and holding on to one another knowing that if we let go we would both collapse. Then I turned around and there sat my three boys, all in tears, and that broke my heart even more.

I remember Jamie telling me, "There are so many people here to see you. Do you want to talk to them?"

But I just sat there staring at the TV not talking to anyone; it was like I was in a trance. At the time, I wasn't able to express my appreciation for all the support and love we received, but I hope everyone knew how much we appreciated it.

The next day we went to my parents' house and my aunts were there helping, but moreso, they were taking control of things knowing my folks were not able to. Normal tasks were a thing of the past at this point and someone had to be their minds and bodies, at least for a while.

Seeing my mom and dad made my pain worse. They were hurting so badly, it broke my heart and all I could do was to think:

How can I fix this?

How do I make them feel better?

Will they ever be happy again?

Will they ever stop crying?

Chad took on a lot of the responsibility of getting things ready for the funeral. I thanked God for him because he apparently saw that the rest of us simply were not going to be able; I couldn't even be alone without breaking down and crying.

Brett and Lauryn came and that was heart-wrenching. Their father was gone and I thought to myself; please someone help them understand why he did this, help us all to understand. Brett was 13 and Lauryn was 11. They will have to live the rest of their lives without their father and I felt a deep, deep sadness for them.

The children wanted to go to his house and get some things they had left there on a previous visit. Jamie, his friends, and my uncle had already been there and had removed Eric's belongings (we were so thankful for that), so I took the kids and Sara but waited in the car while they went inside. As I sat there, I started crying and shaking and asking aloud, "Why Eric, why? We would have done anything for you. Why did you do this?"

The day of the funeral was a long day. So many people came and there were so many flowers, but I told Jamie, "I don't want to be here, I don't want to see people, I don't want to hug anyone or be hugged—I want to be anywhere but here."

I tried so hard to be strong for Mom and Dad. I remember watching them standing in line greeting people; Dad looking so frail, and Mom being so strong and talking with everyone. By now, we were all mentally and physically exhausted, still trying to come to terms with the fact that Eric was gone. We were asking ourselves:

What did we miss? What could we have done differently?

I just wish Eric had known how many people cared about him and maybe it would have helped.

It has now been seven years and I miss my big brother every day. The pain is still there, the image of that day is still there, and I look at my parents and still see the hurt in their eyes.

I have never been mad at Eric for what some may see as a selfish act, for I know had he been himself, he would never have done what he did. My dad and I have both researched Chronic Traumatic Encephalopathy and the effect it has on a person. I believe that all of the head injuries Eric had from playing sports played a significant role in him committing suicide.

Eric was my big brother, someone I love and miss so much. I have great memories of him. Like the time when I was little and I fell and hurt my leg, he carried me inside. I will never forget how safe I felt in his arms and the realization then that he actually did care about his little sister. We are so lucky that we have Brett and Lauryn, whom we can share stories like this with. We tell them, "You two were the most important things in his life and he loved you so very, very much."

Are we okay after all this time? No. But we are all trying even though we will never know or understand why he felt suicide was his only answer. That doesn't change the fact that we love him and miss him.

I have guilt. I think we all do. Honestly, we never thought, like so many other people that have lost someone to suicide, that it would never happen to us. I just know that the mental health system needs to change and that is what I am most mad about. We asked—*begged*—for help, and we *never* got it. Now, we have gone from a family of five to a family of four.

CHAPTER 5

THE FUTURE

It has now been seven years since that terrible day and not a day has gone by that we have not thought about Eric. You never get over losing someone you love, you just have to learn how to get through each day without them.

Time has no significance and cannot determine when the sadness will leave, when we will feel normal again, and when we will rid ourselves of the guilt we have knowing we failed him. There is no such time table.

There are some days (birthdays, holidays, and the date of his death) that are so difficult and the pain is so bad that we don't know how we will ever get over not having him to talk to, to laugh with, or simply to ask his advice on an issue—we thought he knew something about everything!

We miss the "quirky look" he would give us when one of us said something crazy, the way he would clear his throat before he would speak and how he would throw his head back when he laughed—so many memories of him. They are so painful, yet so comforting.

Not long ago I ran into a high school classmate of Eric's and she said to me, "I want you and Bob to know that when it was our high school graduation, I wanted more than anything to walk with Eric in the ceremony. We had grown up together, you were friends with my mom and dad, and I wanted to end our high school years just as we had started our kindergarten years—together. I knew every girl in our class was wondering who he would ask to walk with him and I was sure he would ask one of the more popular girls, but to my surprise and joy, he asked me! I just want you both to know how happy that made me."

Another time, we were at a funeral and a young man came up to us and told us, "I miss Eric so much! We used to have the most fun hanging out and listening to music. There was a song that he really liked and when we would hear it, we would start singing with it. I sure do miss him."

He told us the name of the song but it was one we had never heard of and we have both forgotten what it was.

Bob and I just looked at the young man with tears in our eyes, not knowing he and Eric had ever been friends. I spoke for both of us when I said to him, "Thank you for telling us that. We miss him too."

We often hear stories like this from others who knew him either from school or from working with him. He touched so many lives in so many ways, but he never knew how special he was to so many people.

It saddens us when we read the headlines that another person has committed suicide and it is especially worrisome for the number of young people who are turning to suicide for what they think is the answer to their problems. Suicide has become a serious health problem among all age groups.

Eric was a high achiever, as are many people who die by suicide. He was used to rising above and being the best of the best but he couldn't beat the emotional and physical suffering that was now controlling his life. He started withdrawing from family and friends, drinking more, experiencing more paranoia, and becoming more depressed.

Most people who commit suicide exhibit one or more warning signs, either through what they say or what they do. Eric lived by himself and while we made sure he had his medications and asked him if he was taking them, you can never be sure unless you are with them 24/7. We all checked on Eric daily, tried to interact with him, and reassured him by letting him know we were there for him, but that wasn't enough.

Eric was being treated for depression, the most common condition associated with suicide and often misdiagnosed or untreated. Along with being treated for depression, Eric was being treated for bipolar disorder and schizophrenia;

all contributing factors to him committing suicide. While it was never proven, we believe Chronic Traumatic Encephalopathy (CTE) also played a part in what drove him to feel suicide was his only relief from the physical and mental pain he was feeling.

xxxxx

SUICIDE IN MISSOURI: WHERE WE STAND

- Suicide was the second leading cause of death in Missouri among 10-34 year olds and the fourth leading cause of death among 35-54 year olds. On average, one person dies by suicide every eight hours in Missouri *(Missouri Department of Mental Health, 2016)*.

- One out of eight (12%) middle school students seriously considered suicide in the past year, 9% planned, and 6% attempted suicide *(Missouri Department of Health, 2018)*.

- Among high school students, one in six (16%) seriously considered suicide, 13% planned a suicide, and 6% attempted suicide. Ideation rates for females were higher than for males (18% vs. 10%) *(Missouri Department of Health, 2018)*.

- One in five college students (21%) reported seriously considering suicide in the past year *(Missouri Department of Health, 2018)*.

- Full-time college students ages 18-22 were less likely to attempt suicide than others their age *(National Study for Drug Use and Health, 2019)*.

- LGBTQ students were more than two times more likely to have had suicidal thoughts than non-LGBTQ students and were nearly five times as likely to have made a suicide attempt (41% vs. 18%) *(Missouri Department of Health, 2018)*.

xxxxx

For those who think that the only way to end their pain is to end their life, then they need to go to the cemetery with a father and mother who just buried their child—no pain can be compared to this. While the one who ended their life also ended their pain, there is no ending for the family because their pain will go on incessantly.

In May of 2017, we attended Eric's son's graduation from high school. Brett is tall (6'7") and handsome—resembling his father in his looks, mannerisms, and his blue eyes. In May of 2018, we attended his daughter's high school graduation. Beautiful Lauryn, with her long legs, long brown hair, and brown eyes—the spitting image of her mother.

As we sat and watched each of these two amazing young adults accept their diplomas, all we could do was to think how sad it was that their father was not there to see them. Eric is not only missing the little everyday memories, but he is missing all of the big ones as well: their proms, high school and college graduations, walking his daughter down the aisle, and his first grandchild.

We are thankful that Eric's children still spend time with us whenever they can. We know they will eventually outgrow us, but we hope for the times they do come we create many happy memories for them, memories they will always treasure. They are a part of Eric and we are thankful for every minute we can spend with them.

CHAPTER 6

BRETT'S STORY

"He shall wipe every tear from their eyes. There will be no more death or mourning or crying or pain, for the old order of things has passed away."

Revelations 21:4

I have an immense amount of pride in saying that Eric Varner is my dad. From as early as I can remember, he was nothing but a kind-hearted man. He would never like to hurt any living thing. Whenever there was a spider in our house, he would trap it and set it free outside (whereas most people would simply kill it).

Whenever it would get close to Christmas time, he would take me with him to buy toys for families who were less fortunate than us, and he would always give the homeless people off the exit ramp of the Interstate cash if he had it. I must admit I didn't appreciate his thoughtfulness until years later.

Growing up with him as my father gave me a lot to live up to. When we would go visit my family in Unionville, Missouri, everyone would talk about how athletically gifted and successful he was. He always pushed me to play as many sports as I could and I am very glad he did (although I did not like all of them).

A couple years down the road, I noticed my parents had started fighting and my father had spurts where he would act very out of character. I was still pretty young so I didn't think anything of it.

Later, my parents got a divorce and I stopped seeing my dad as frequently because he moved back to Unionville. He always made sure to call me every night, even though I couldn't always answer. I still have some of the voicemails that he left. I cherish them more than anything because I never realized how lucky I was to be able to hear his voice, until I no longer could.

My sister and I always enjoyed going to visit him at the lake. We would have our cousins over and go swimming in the cove. One of my favorite memories there was during the winter time when the lake was frozen over. My cousin had a remote control car and we were driving it around on the frozen lake. Before long the batteries died, and the car was stuck out of reach on the frozen lake.

After discussing the problem with Dad, he went into the house, then came back with an extension cord. After several attempts to lasso the car, he finally managed to get the extension cord around the car, and pulled the car into shore—all the while my cousin and I were about to die from laughter.

When we went out in public, I started noticing his paranoia getting progressively worse. He would think people were staring at him or following us in the car. I knew something was wrong with him, but I didn't think it was very serious or that it would last long because he seemed normal most of the time when we were with him.

I didn't have him close to home to push me athletically anymore, so I stopped playing sports. It wasn't until my freshman year of high school that I decided to try out for the football team. I had always looked up to him and his football career, so I started playing football because I wanted to be like him—even though he always told me I needed to be playing basketball because I was so tall.

On March 22, 2012, my whole world was flipped upside down. I had seen my mom crying that evening and family friends would come to the house and talk to her with concerned expressions. But, I continued to play outside. Later that night, she sat my sister and me down on the couch and said with tears falling from her eyes, "I don't know how to say this, but there's been an accident and your dad is dead."

All I could think of was:

Why?

Why couldn't I have talked to him?

Why couldn't I have gone up to visit him sooner?

Why did he do this?

Every phone call I missed from him came flashing back now and the guilt overwhelmed me.

Everything was a blur until the funeral. That's when things began to sink in. Looking up to see my dad in his casket was the hardest thing I have ever forced myself to do. I remember walking to him and saying our last goodbyes after the service. I couldn't force myself to touch his hand because I didn't want anything that had just happened to be real.

That year, I began playing basketball again, like he'd always wanted me to do. But it was too late; I would never get to have him in the bleachers watching me.

Now every accomplishment I have made will never be as sweet knowing that he isn't there watching. I'd do anything to make him proud of me one more time.

Growing up the rest of my life without my dad isn't very easy. I no longer have someone to talk to from a fatherly perspective, I can't shoot hoops with Dad, or play catch with him anymore, and I can no longer ask for his guidance.

To this day, I still miss him more than ever. I just remember our times in the back patio playing horse in basketball and how good I had it. I think of how much I took it for granted. Although he is gone, my memory of him will live on.

Every time I hear the word suicide, I wince a little just thinking of the pain that person was going through and the pain of the family. I still would give anything to speak with him one more time, I have so many questions for him, but I guess they'll have to wait. You never know what you have until it's gone.

CHAPTER 7

LAURYN'S STORY

We all know that the bond between a father and son is special. The son is the father's legacy—to carry on the family name. The bond between father and daughter is also special. It is protective, gentle, and brings out the softer side of a father that most people don't often see. I was privileged enough to have that bond with my dad, Eric Varner.

Dad loved Brett so much, that was obvious. He was the first child and a son at that. But, being the little girl, I was the "apple of his eye" and I knew it! I often got away with things that I probably shouldn't have (and I more than once took advantage of that).

His pet name for me was "Piggit." *What an awful name* I  used to think. *Why couldn't he have picked one such as cupcake, princess, or another "girly" name.* But no, I was Piggit! I am not sure how that name came about. He used to read me the book *Winnie the Pooh* and my favorite character was Piglet; so at first that is what he called me: Piglet. With time, that got shortened and Dad's pet name for me eventually ended up as Piggit. When he would call me that, I would whine and moan and tell him, "Don't call me that." But all the while, I knew it was his special name for me and I loved it!

Trying to write something for my part of the story was anything but easy. I struggled putting my feelings and memories of my dad into words. He was so special, he loved me to the moon and back, and I loved him the same.

Knowing I needed more to my story, I decided to use some posts I had put on Facebook at different times in honor of Dad. They say everything about the man and father that Eric Varner was:

FATHER'S DAY POST

"To the strongest, most affectionate, compassionate man I know. Happy Father's Day to the only man to love me almost as much as God. Without you, I wouldn't be half as strong, independent, or as caring as I am today. I could never find the words to thank you for that. We all love and miss you, Dad. Happy Father's Day, my angel."

BIRTHDAY POSTS

"I used to be his angel, now he is mine. Happy Birthday, Daddy."

"The strongest girls have a loved one in heaven."

"Today is one of my most fondest memories of my dad..." "Today, you would be 49 and probably binge eating Reese's peanut butter chip cookies that I had failed at attempting to make. We would probably go to an old diner for lunch and you would overstuff on meatloaf, or we would go sit in the park with KFC. Your birthday was always one of my favorite days. I feel as if this day has never fallen on a day when it was rainy or cloudy.

We would probably be laughing at baby videos and dog videos—your two favorite things. Gosh, what I would give to hear you laugh at those silly commercials again. Your laugh has always been my favorite and your bright blue eyes. I will have the most beautiful dreams sometimes about you and your eyes are always the brightest thing in my dream.

Thank you for teaching me strength, independence, and to love myself. But most of all strength. It has been almost 6 1/2 years since you escaped into heaven and I still miss you every day. Days like today are days that test my strength but every second I overcome it, I get a little bit stronger. You make me stronger everyday and I thank you for that.

You allowed me to grow up quickly and see that the world is not always rainbows and butterflies. I could never thank you enough for that.

You have given me the greatest gift I could ever receive and that is how to love a person you can't see or touch anymore but I know you are there, I feel you. Happy 49th birthday, Daddy, my guardian angel."

"Thank you for being the angel on my shoulder now. Gone Too Soon!"

Depression is a monster of a disease. Never make permanent decisions based on a temporary situation. I promise there are people who want to help you, just let them. #inlovingmemoryofEricVarner my dad!"

"Happy birthday. I love and miss you so much."

CHAPTER 8

SARA'S STORY:
My Husband, EV

"Loving you changed my life. It should come as no surprise that losing you has done the same."

Chloe Frayne

It was 1994. I was just returning to my hometown after college to take my first job. I had dreamed of a glamorous job somewhere far, far away in a big, beautiful, bustling city, but here I was. Back at home. I wanted to be anywhere in the world but there. Small town, USA. It was the last place on earth I dreamed of finding the perfect job. It was the kind of town where everyone knew your business and if they didn't, they'd tell everyone they did anyway. Seriously... anywhere else! I wanted to be anywhere else in the world but Chillicothe, Missouri!

But then, out of the blue, in walked Eric Varner. He was new in town. He had a great job, he was responsible, charming and oh, so handsome! He was the total package. All of a sudden, I was exactly where I wanted to be.

Everyone, and I mean everyone, loved Eric. When I think of meeting Eric for the first time, I think of those twinkling blue eyes, and his laughter, and that ornery sparkle he would get when teasing me! He was good natured, fun, he loved Jesus, and was proud to tell me so on our very first date. Oh, I was in love! I was head over heels. He was a dream come true. Picture perfect.

We were happy together. We were married after dating for ten months. We had our peaks and valleys like any newlyweds. But for the most part, it was good. Eric played softball and I would follow along to the ball fields to watch him play in his signature red shoes. His buddies all lovingly referred to him as "EV". He was my #21 and I loved to watch him play. Our phone number even ended in -0021.

Early in our marriage, we took a trip together to Graceland and we both fell in love with Elvis. Eric was not an emotional person very often. Music was his avenue for emotional expression. Elvis music and the Braveheart soundtrack were among his most favorite, but he had a wide variety of music preferences depending on his mood.

I absolutely loved Eric's ornery side. He always thought it was great fun to bang on the bathroom door really loudly when you were inside. It was so loud, you couldn't help but scream, even though you could totally hear him coming because he could never sneak up on anyone with his ankles that popped with each step—thanks to years of football and various injuries. He would laugh out loud when we would scream.

As time went on, both of our careers began to evolve and take off. In 2002, Eric had the fantastic opportunity to transfer to Cape Girardeau. Six hours away made it seem like it was across the world. By this time, we had two children and the support in my hometown was very hard to leave. I begrudgingly agreed. But if and only if:

1. I got a job I liked.

2. We could sell our house.

As it turned out, I got two amazing job offers and our house sold within 3 days. I didn't want to hold him back and there was way more career opportunity in Cape, so we packed up the kids and our lives in a big U-Haul truck and left home behind on a pouring rainy Memorial Day weekend.

Cape was great. We loved it there. We had a gorgeous home, amazing friends, fantastic daycare options for the kids, the schools were amazing, and it felt like a dream. Less than six months after moving there, Eric got another even better job as a sales representative with a small Japanese pharmaceutical company called Eisai. We were truly living the dream. Everything seemed perfect! Eric was a mover and a shaker and he was on track for rapid promotion in his company. But change was coming. Not too long in his tenure with Eisai, Eric was involved in a vehicle crash. He suffered whiplash and back and neck pain as a result. He began taking narcotics to help manage his pain.

Three years after we moved to Cape, we took a dream vacation to Mexico with two other couples to celebrate our ten year wedding anniversary. It was then that I realized something wasn't quite right with Eric. I had been noticing we were receiving bills charged to his credit card that just didn't make sense. When I asked him about them, he brushed them off at first. It was my job to manage the money in our checking accounts and pay the bills. After my questioning, he stopped letting me see the credit card statements and would only leave me with the billing slip. He would avoid my questions.

Later, I learned that he was spending sometimes between $600 and $700 per month consulting with 'doctors' in Florida and Canada. He was purchasing mail-order opioids from pharmacies out of the country. Then when we were in Mexico, it seemed that the most important thing to him was going to the pharmacies.

His friend asked, "what's the deal?" But Eric was vague: "They have cheap medications." I cornered him after the trip. He eventually confessed that he had a lot of pain and his doctors were prescribing him Hydrocodone.

I went along to various doctor appointments with him as he struggled to find someone who could help him figure out what was wrong. I remember on one doctor visit, the doctor told him his pain was psychosomatic—it was all made up in his head. Eric was furious. He went to more doctors and got pain medications. He continued to use more and more. Many times he tried to quit them, which resulted in several trips to the Emergency Room.

I called his friend one night when he had clearly taken too much. I didn't understand the symptoms of overdose at the time, but his friend's advice was, "Just make sure he keeps breathing."

Eric took too much on several occasions and his behavior scared me. He fell off the ladder to our son's bunk bed one night while tucking him in and passed out. I stayed awake, terrified, to watch him breathe.

I remember one day that he demanded I go to the pharmacy for him and get his medications; they wouldn't give them to him because it was too soon for a refill. The pharmacist was less than friendly to me about the situation when I inquired as to why Eric couldn't get his medication. I didn't understand it but as time went on, it became increasingly clearer that he had an opioid problem.

I felt like a ship at sea. We were all alone and we were drowning. There didn't seem to be anywhere to turn. No one seemed to understand what was going on and I certainly didn't. There was minimal information on the internet at the time so I didn't know where to go for help or what to do. So, we just kept going, quietly, day after day.

Eric was my biggest cheerleader. And the best part was, he truly believed in me. Much more so than I did myself. I loved my job as a school counselor with the Jackson School District, but I was getting restless. I had done the same job for nearly 10 years and I was ready to try something new. I always dreamed of becoming a pharmaceutical representative. And when Eric began working as a rep, it made me want it even more. It looked like such a fun and rewarding job to me. He was totally on board and supported me with every step. He was a great encourager. He empowered me, pushed me, and cheered me on as I applied, interviewed, and got rejected...time after time.

Until finally, in 2007, I found the job I had only dreamed of. Without his support and encouragement, I would never have been brave or strong enough to chase my dream. It truly was a dream come true. I'm still so thankful in my heart every single day that he believed in me and helped me achieve my dream.

Once I started my new job, I began to notice that Eric didn't seem to be going to work. I would come home in the middle of the day and his car would be parked in my space in the garage with the door shut, as if to hide his vehicle. He was disengaged from our family and spent lots of time watching TV or his favorite movies: Braveheart, Gladiator, and others. He often stayed up all night and slept during the day.

Six months after I started my job, Eric came to me and said he needed to resign before he was fired. He told me his boss was "out to get him" and he needed to quit. He believed his boss was having him followed. I trusted and supported him completely. But I had a pain in my gut and I knew that things were not right. Eric applied for multiple jobs and was the front runner for several amazing jobs, but time and time again, he was not the one they hired. He was crushed.

Eric was a man of great compassion for others. His career was not moving forward as it had been, but he didn't let that stop him. Eric immersed himself in doing things that would help others. He had a passion for our servicemen and servicewomen. He involved himself with Operation Homefront, a national organization focused on helping families of service members in need of basic things like housing and utilities. Eric had a tremendously loving heart for the kids in those families and he took on the role of soliciting donations and purchasing toys for children of military families for Christmas. He had a heart of gold.

I don't really remember when the odd behaviors started happening. It was a little thing said here or there, or an occasional odd admission to paranoia. It was easy to brush off at first.

Then for Eric's 40th birthday in December of 2008, I hosted a surprise party for him at Buffalo Wild Wings. I was so excited and I had planned it out for months, creating the perfect invitation, arranging for some of his favorite things, and coordinating with his family and friends.

We had an amazing celebration. The day came and went without a hitch! Or so I thought. There was a hitch. A *big* one. Eric was surprised; he was very surprised. He had no idea in advance that there would be a party. I felt so proud that I had pulled it off and he got to see everyone there to celebrate with him. It seemed like such a success. But, after the party cleared out and everyone went home, Eric was furious. He was furious *with me*. How had I done all of this without him knowing anything or having any idea that his family was coming from far away? I got him to the restaurant under false pretenses!

I'll admit I probably wasn't entirely truthful with him to coordinate everything and get him there on time. But it seemed a small thing to me because I was planning this out of love for him; I truly thought he would love it and be appreciative. But he didn't and he wasn't. He *hated* it. He was angry like I'd never seen. He felt lied to, misled, betrayed. I really pulled one over on him. I got him good!

I was shocked by his reaction. How could he be angry at me for this? I thought I did a good thing. I was truly trying to celebrate my husband and make him feel loved. He didn't think so at all. After that night, I noticed he was suspicious of me. Did I really go to Walmart? The grocery store? A meeting after work? Was I meeting someone? Were my intentions good or was I up to something? There was a nagging sense that the suspicion was always there.

Gradually, his behavior became more and more noticeable. Eventually, I couldn't ignore that something had to be done. In June of 2009, we went on a beach vacation with my family in North Carolina. There were about a dozen of my family members with us in a beach house. The first night we were there, Eric woke me in the middle of the night. He wanted me to come outside with him. I was reluctant because we had traveled all day. I was exhausted and it was 2 or 3 A.M. But he was incessant, so I agreed thinking there must be an animal like a raccoon or something he wanted to show me (Eric loved animals, so this would not have surprised me at all). But when he got me outside, he did surprise me. He was angry. He told me that the house was bugged with cameras. That my parents had put hidden cameras everywhere before we arrived. I laughed; I thought it was completely ridiculous. I remember laughing and telling him, "My parents don't know how to run the remote to their TV! There's no way they put cameras in this house!" It seemed so absurd to me, but Eric was serious. He was adamant and there was no convincing him that there were no cameras. He believed we were all watching him because we thought he was stealing my Aunt's medications which were lined up in the bathroom.

When I realized he was serious and he truly believed all of this, I got scared. But I knew I had to do something. I spent the rest of that week lying awake and trying to come up with a plan. When we returned home, I left for work on Monday morning. I went straight to Eric's primary care doctor, and I told him the story. He told me that Eric absolutely must get off the opioids and see a psychiatrist immediately. Reluctantly, I approached Eric with this news, knowing that I might be walking onto a land mine. And it turns out that I was. He was furious with my meddling and betrayal. He immediately went to the doctor and changed his HIPAA paperwork. So from then on, I was shut out of all of his healthcare. I was devastated. My plan was destroyed and now things were worse, not better.

Eric began keeping me up all night going through the same phone bills. Wanting to know why various cell phone towers were sending messages to my phone. He demanded to know who I was seeing. It was no one. I was barely functioning in life, let alone having the time or the energy for an affair. I would leave for work and come back home to another sleepless night of talking through phone bills and mysterious text messages. I would convince him he was imagining all of this, and he seemed to finally understand. This behavior seemed to come in waves. It would be fine for a few weeks, but then a switch would flip and it was as if we never even had a conversation about it; it would all begin again. It was unbearable.

The more his mental health deteriorated, the more suspicious he became of me. He would become so enraged at times that I became fearful. He believed I was having multiple affairs. He believed I was bugging his vehicle, the light bulbs, the electrical outlets, and the microwave in our home. He believed I was having him followed. In public, he would yell at strangers that he thought were following him. He would threaten the neighbors or families of the men with whom he believed I was having affairs.

His behavior became more and more out of control. He was taking narcotics, sleep medicines, and using alcohol. The combination was terrifying at times. I was fearful of his accusations and anger toward me. In a second, his captivating blue eyes would become black and expressionless. He was fine one minute and would flip 180 degrees without provocation; it was like we had never resolved any of these issues before. But we had resolved all of these things, or so I thought.

Sometimes it was the same thing all night long, night after night, for several nights in a row. It was utterly exhausting. I would get up the next morning, get the kids to school, go to work. Then I would come home, fix dinner, do homework and bath time with the kids, and do it all again. I didn't know what to do or where to turn. I tried to keep our family life as "normal" as I possibly could. But whenever I could find a chance, I spent hours on the internet, trying to figure out what was going on and what to do about it. But I found nothing. There was no help. I didn't want to embarrass him by talking to people about it. It destroyed our marriage and eventually, we divorced.

Eric adored his children. He was an amazing father. But as his illness took over, he was not able to care for them as he wanted to and needed to. I think he knew his limitations and he seldom took the kids when it was "his weekend." When he did take them, he would generally only take one at a time for just a couple hours. He absolutely loved his children with his whole heart and was a loving father, but it was hard for him to manage the stress of the two of them together because his mind was not in a good place. They were busy, normal kids that liked to be silly and fuss with each other a lot. He felt irritable and agitated, but he never wanted to act that way in front of them. He hated this because his children were the absolute most important thing in this world to him. Losing time with them was devastating to him.

It was Labor Day weekend about a month after our divorce was final when he contacted his friend, Jeff, and tried to get him to go downtown with him. Jeff declined. A couple days later, Jeff called me to let me know that Eric had gone downtown that weekend alone and that he had been in a physical altercation. Eric had broken ribs and had contusions; he had been left unconscious on the sidewalk. He was picked up by Cape PD. It was at this point, I knew I was of no help to Eric and he needed the support of his family. I contacted his brother and asked him to come get him and take him home where he would have support and people looking after him whom he trusted. God bless Chad and his wife, for coming. I have no idea how he convinced Eric to go home, but he did.

Sadly, I feared for a very long time that Eric would ultimately end his own life. Trying to stop it was like trying to stop a train. How he survived as long as he did is amazing to me. He was truly a warrior, fighting a battle. He was valiant. He was a braveheart.

The illness was too much for anyone, but Eric fought harder than I ever could have imagined. Even though I expected it, nothing could ever prepare me to hear those words on the phone from Chad. I believe Eric just wanted his pain to end. I certainly cannot blame him for that. Eric's pain was enormous and unfathomable. He deserves no fault for wanting that to end. I think that's what we all wanted for him, but not that way.

I don't think he understood that the pain doesn't end when you end your own life. You merely hand it over to everyone you love and let them carry it. It leaves them broken, trying to pick up the pieces of their lives and find a way to cope. And they spend their time trying to make sense of the unsolvable mystery.

Why?

Not one of us who loved him had ever experienced anything like this before. Not one of us knew which way to turn, what to do, how to fix it, or how to stop it. If any one of us could have changed it, *every single one of us* would have. We all got a membership card to a club that no one ever wants to be a part of. There is not one of us that is okay with the way it ended.

The grief was an ocean at first: black, enormous, and all-consuming. It was followed by tidal waves of grief with little pieces of life in between. The waves just keep coming; they never really stop. Small ones, big ones, and everything in between. But gradually as time goes on, there are more pieces of life in between. Time has a way of forcing you to move on. Kids grow up. Things change. But sometimes the waves catch you unprepared. They show up when they're least expected. Seven years later, something as simple as a melody playing at the grocery store, or an innocent comment by a stranger, or seeing Eric's children in a moment he should be seeing for himself, can conjure an emotion so powerful it can nearly bring me to my knees.

Truly I think Eric thought he was doing the right thing for the people he loved. He didn't want to be a burden to anyone. But, he truly had no idea what a burden his absence would be to those of us he left behind.

I can't help but think that if Eric or I knew what was going on with him or with his mind, we both would have been better equipped to deal with it. We would have made better decisions in helping him get the care he needed. But as it was, neither of us knew what that was. It cost us our relationship. Mental illnesses are so complex. When there is something wrong with your heart or other organs, there are medical procedures and medications to help. When there is something wrong with your brain, it manifests in behaviors which make it much more challenging to identify and treat.

I complained about his depression because I didn't know that's what it was. I didn't know that's why he wouldn't come out of the basement and participate in life with our growing and busy family. I didn't know that's why he wouldn't go to work, or take out the trash, or mow the grass, or mail the bills I had written out and left on the kitchen table for him. I reacted with irritation and frustration that I was the only one in the house carrying the load for a family of four. He thought I was griping and complaining all the time, I thought he was being lazy. He looked just fine on the outside. But now I know he wasn't fine on the inside. Not at all.

I didn't understand how much he wanted to participate in our lives and be a part of it all. I wish I would have done many, many things differently. Today as I write this, I have the curse that comes with hindsight: 20/20 vision. But when you're in the middle of mental illness, there is no ability to see the forest for the trees.

In Eric's case, I believe CTE may have contributed to his mental health struggles. That condition, along with opioid use seems to have been a disastrous combination. In addition to the behavioral and emotional health issues, Eric began to occasionally have an unsteady gait. He would fall and hurt himself.

I remember one day, we took the kids to Johnson Shut Ins. It's a beautiful Missouri state park with a creek that flows through a rocky area, leaving little pools and streams of water where people can swim and play. He was having an angry day—as he often did when we tried to travel or go anywhere together. He was hopping from rock to rock and jumping great distances on the slippery rocks. I commented that I was worried about him jumping so far on the wet, slippery rocks. Eventually, he did slip and hurt his shin terribly. I felt so bad for him but he was being so angry that day he didn't get the sympathy he deserved.

He just seemed so overconfident in his physical abilities at that moment. There were other times when I would notice a stagger or misstep. His hands would occasionally shake with tremors or just unsteadiness. It's hard to put a finger on, but something just wasn't entirely right. Eric suffered multiple concussions during his football career. Additionally in 2007, he sustained another concussion while at the skate park with the kids. He fell and hit his head so hard that he was knocked unconscious. He never sought treatment and I never knew anything about it until months after the fact. The car accident he was involved in around that time may have also been a significant contributing factor.

Sometimes I hear Eric in my son's laugh or in his voice as he's gotten older, the way he talks, things he says, or the way he does something and it makes me miss Eric so much. Brett sounds so much like him on the phone. Or I see him in Lauryn's kind and positive nature, and in her enthusiasm for people and life. The thrill and joy in her voice when you give her a gift. He had that too. It made me love giving him gifts. I see so much of his goodness in her too. He is certainly a huge part of both of our children.

I believe with better resources for mental health, our story would have been very different. At the end of the day, my hope and my prayer is that stories like Eric's lead to better mental health with sweeter endings.

CHAPTER 9

CLINT'S STORY

"Varner, I will never judge you for what you did because I know how much pain you were feeling. I'll never blame you for what you did. I just wish every day that you never felt that you had to take your own life to escape the pain. I know it wasn't an easy decision. I know it wasn't your decision. You never let me down before. I miss you every day. I'm so sorry I let you down."
Clint Crain

The setting was a hot, muggy morning in August of 1988 during one of three college football practices in full football gear. You know one of those days where on the radio, farmers are being warned to take special care of their livestock due to excessive heat. I'm a freshman away from home for the first time and I'm getting my ass kicked by grown men each day. I'm dead tired and at this point, I don't have a friend on the football team. Classes have not started as our team is preparing for the football season. It was the first time I noticed Eric "Bird" Varner.

In college, we all had nicknames. Mine was Rat—don't ask. You either were called the nickname or your last name. I'm not sure I've called my buddy "Eric" more than 25 times in all the years we have known each other. Anyway I could go on and on about college, but I know as I write, Bird is looking down on me: *Rat don't do it!* He is worried about the stories I'll tell. To be fair, he has *many* stories on me!

Varner had confidence; that would be an understatement. But if you are good, why not be cocky? Varner was a sophomore who if you didn't know it, you would think he was a senior and the captain of our football team by the way he carried himself on the field. Everyone on that football field knew Varner. I knew at that time, he was a special football player. What I didn't know is he would become to mean as much to me as family. We were like brothers. We were lucky to have a group of friends/teammates that would do anything for us. Varner was known and liked by all.

College was special for me because of the friendships. Varner is at the top of the list. For many years, we were together 24/7. We had so much fun, so many laughs, and so many conversations. Conversations where you get to know someone's soul. Our friends and teammates were notorious for giving each other a hard time (trust me, there were no boundaries). The weak did not last long with us. I can remember playing pool in "establishments," giving each other grief, and guys who did not know us would ask,

"Are you guys going to fight?"

"Hell no! But don't chime in on one of our pals."

I remember being broke most of my college life. I remember loaning money to a few guys and never seeing it again. I also remember not loaning money to a few guys. The first time Varner asked to borrow money, he said he would pay me back by _____. He did. Varner's word was his word. I could *always* count on him.

After college we had to grow up...kind of. Varner became a liquor control agent with the State of Missosuri. Yeah, *that guy*. He was really good at it, but something wonderful happened: he met Sara. Eric didn't want to be an agent with a family. He wanted the best for his family. He changed professions and became a pharmaceutical sales representative. I was so impressed with his accomplishments in pharmaceutical sales. You must be smart and understand sales to achieve success in that field. I wish I would have told him how proud I was of him in his pharmaceutical sales career.

Eric grew up in a time where the mindset in football was: "Rub a little dirt on your injury. Get back out there.

There are 100 guys who want your job. Is this the moment that you're going to choose to be weak and let everyone down?" I witnessed this mindset from him during Varner's senior year in college. He fractured his ankle midseason. He knew he would not receive a medical redshirt. He wanted to finish the season he started and he didn't want to let his teammates down. Playing wide receiver, the man taped his ankle up. He participated in every practice and gave 110% effort. On a fractured ankle, not only did he finish the season but he received all-conference. Not many men are "Varner tough"!

I know Eric Varner. He loved life from the moment I met him. He loved his family, friends, and Sara. I know without question how much he loved Brett and Lauryn. Eric would talk about his kids to me often. He was so proud of Brett and Lauryn.

Eric had an amazing family and career. He had it all. I watched Eric lose his career and then his wife; he moved away from Brett and Lauryn. Eric was competitive, smart, and a real family man. How could someone go from the top of the mountain to the bottom so quickly?

When Eric returned to Unionville, we would talk almost every night. He would tell me the extreme pain he was experiencing. I did not know how to help. Instead, I listened and offered advice. When all else failed, I'd make him laugh. I could always make him laugh. Eric said things that were not healthy. He told me what he was thinking of doing. I made him promise me he would not do it. He promised me he would not and the deal was: he would call me. He would always call me. I trusted him, just as I always have for all these years. The man I knew and loved would *not* break a promise to me. The man I knew could deal with pain. He would overcome the pain.

A time came where I knew I needed to go see Varner at the lake. The night started as it always did: a bro hug, "dogging" each other (making fun of each other), and catching up on family. Varner wanted me to meet a few of his buddies from high school, so we went to their house. After about 30 minutes, he wanted to leave. For some reason, he wanted to leave me with strangers. He kept making bad excuses as to why he needed to leave; I just had a bad feeling.

I insisted that I was going with him back to his house. Eric was upset, but he agreed for me to leave with him. On the way to his house, he played chicken with another car and became very agitated. Once we settled into his house, we started talking and he was asking me absurd questions. He thought Jeff Appleman and I were hiding information from him. After I continued to say, "I don't know and Duck does not know," Eric pulled a gun out and pointed it at my head. The gun was pointed at my head for roughly ten minutes as he continued to ask me questions. I had no choice but to trust he would put the gun down. I know he was in pain. I believe no matter what that he would never hurt me, no matter what state of mind.

After Eric put the gun down, it is kind of a blur. I ended up at Bob and Sue Ann's home. We, along with the Sheriff, went to Eric's. The plan was to have him committed. We just hoped this would help him. Eric was not pleased with our decision; he was very upset. I'll never forget the way he looked at me. He said, "If Crain says I need to go, I'll go." I said, "Yes."

The look on his face broke my heart. He left and I heard about it after his release from the mental treatment center. Eric gave me a piece of his mind for about ten minutes and like all other disagreements we had over the years, it was in the past. He promised me he would get help. We continued talking almost every night until I had a neck surgery. The surgery had a complication and we were unable to speak for about 8 days. Once we connected after my surgery, I had no idea it would be our last conversation; I'll never forget it. During the time Eric was having problems, I could not figure out what happened to my friend. I now have a theory.

CTE: confusion, impaired judgement, impulse control problems, aggression, depression, anxiety, suicidality. Unfortunately, Eric checks all the boxes. When we played football, receiving a concussion was a badge of honor.

There isn't a day that goes by where I don't think about Varner. Every day, I feel responsible for what happened to Eric.

Brett, Lauryn, and the Varner family,

I'm so sorry I failed Eric. I knew him well. He loved you all and he was a great man.

CHAPTER 10

JEFF'S STORY
Troubadour

It is with great honor to give my perspective on the life and tragic death of a man who was more like a brother to me than a friend, Eric Gaberiel Varner. Although we met in our late teenage years, I had the unique vantage point of seeing him develop from a young college athletic jock to a God-fearing father of two. He became a true professional in the pharmaceutical and the world of medical sales. He was a classic car enthusiast who had an infectious smile and laugh that made any event with him a special moment.

I first met Eric in August of 1988, as our paths crossed at Graceland College in Lamoni, Iowa. I reported to football camp as a freshman and was placed in a dorm room on a floor called Stuart Manor. Within the first 24 hours, I introduced myself to some upperclassmen football players who lived adjacent to my room. The formal introduction turned into a wrestling match of sorts with a guy they called "Pup." This unprovoked wrestling match ended up a little heated, tearing up their dorm room as we both declared victory, and a mutual respect was established. To this day, I'm still not sure what instigated the actions of our first encounter, but that rocky start was undoubtedly testosterone fueled by a fearless pigeon-chested teammate known by the last name Varner.

I had never witnessed a guy his size, who was pound-for-pound tough as nails and a complete handful. Fortunately, he took me under his wing and the first week of football camp was in the books. I was quick to realize the admiration other players had for Eric. He was charismatic, chalk full of athleticism—which included speed, strength, and stamina with an insatiable desire to win. He was a great football player and teammate.

During my years at Graceland, my teammate turned into a roommate and we developed a very close circle of friends. Cell phone pictures and videos didn't exist at that time, and I can honestly say we were all creating "made for movie" memories. Fortunately, they could never be duplicated, let alone be believed; most of them will live in perpetuity amongst our circle. Antics and laughter were the preference for this group to say the least.

Nicknames were hard to come by, and if you had one, I will guarantee you did something epic to earn it, and I will have to admit, it's a lifelong designation. Eric was legendary based on nicknames alone. I guess when your personality and talents are so incredible, you start stacking them up. Pup, Pidgeon, Bird, EV, Birdicus were all used interchangeably always invoking a squinty-eye smile from the owner. In later years, his favorite nickname of all was definitely Dad, as he had two incredible kids, Brett and Lauryn whom he loved unconditionally.

Luckily after graduating, we never lost contact with each other despite living in different locations for a period of time. He always surrounded himself with great people wherever he was and lived life to the fullest. Around 2002, Eric moved to the Cape Girardeau, MO area with his wife, Sara, and Brett and Lauryn. It was great to have his family living in the same area as mine. Real life set in on both of us: families, jobs, and never-ending activities. We always found something to talk about or do together. Maturity was an inevitable process we both had to adjust to, even though we could easily switch back to the lack thereof, during college days. Life was great, and we were both blessed beyond comprehension. New homes, stable jobs, great mutual friends, kids, pets: we were living large— surpassing our humble beginnings in a certain yellow house in Lamoni, Iowa.

Varner's changes in behavior began around 2007 to the best of my recollection. No major changes from my perspective; they were subtle in nature. Life stresses and job changes in his industry were most likely the reason. We didn't spend as much time together, but texting and phone calls never stopped. Eric continued to live, work, and play full throttle. He still thought he had super athletic powers despite the many candles accumulating on his yearly cake. I could easily goad him into proving his powers and nothing would irritate him more than calling him out on being able to do a standing backflip. I've seen him do it a hundred times, but the stiffening old man would never shy away from a dare. Needless to say, around this time was the first time I witnessed incomplete rotation. Old and new injuries were occurring, which also added to some of these changes.

These injuries had accumulated during our time at Graceland playing football. Bird was an offensive wide receiver and kickoff and punt returner. The majority of his buddies all played defense. Needless to say, the two sides were mostly separated during practices. That is until the end of practice when we would come together and scrimmage together. Bird was always going hard and constantly looking to deliver big hits. That was a two-way road shared by his buddies on the other side, and I can't even begin to count the collisions I have seen him take and deliver. Post-practice locker room stories and reactions to cheap versus legitimate shots were one of my favorite things to debate. He considered it a badge of courage going over the middle and taking a lick, getting up, and doing it again. He loved the game and the contact. Games were much better, as we would all take great pride in his toughness and his speed, outperforming his mortal coverage guys and getting crushed somewhere downfield. But he always popped back up. Concussions were a part of the game. However back then, you got up and shook the cobwebs out and you were off to the next play.

So, you are probably wondering right now: *what happened to Eric and this American Dream scenario?* My personal observations and medical background will hopefully shed some light: random thoughts and chronic injuries linger forever. Minor injuries sometimes require minor medical or surgical procedures to correct. Pain medications after procedures can be addictive. Breaking addictions is difficult for the majority of those affected. When narcotics are withdrawn, some will resort to other pain-relieving modalities such as alcohol. These thoughts did occur when I considered Eric, but was seen as a small hiccup in his path. He could recover from anything, because he was that kind of guy. Unfortunately, a complete metamorphosis was about to take place that took a toll on his wife and kids.

Personality changes were becoming more noticeable, then neurologic symptoms started to present including hand tremors. Paranoia became problematic, then became total delusions. *What is going on here?*

Eric soon moved in with my family as his marriage was on hold with a formal separation. I knew how much he loved his family, and he started to work harder than ever to preserve it. We would talk all night about what he needed to do to get back to normal. He continued to work and became more distressed on a daily basis. Knowing him for all these years, and having him live in your basement with your family was a little tough to say the least. Regardless, I loved the guy and would help him in any way possible. I knew he wasn't dangerous, and he loved my family like his own. He soon became overwhelmingly convinced someone was making this happen to him. He was positive someone was following him on a daily basis. He became suspicious of everything and everyone.

I suggested we move him to my office apartment and get some professional help. He was seen by multiple psychiatrists. The first one believed what he was saying and offered little help. I suggested he get a second opinion, which he did and that physician had similar views.

Retrospectively, he could turn on and off his Jekyll and Hyde act initially, which most likely fooled the professionals. He continued to formulate wild conspiracies and just wanted to be back with his family. Ultimately, he moved back to Unionville, MO after an altercation at a local bar, where he essentially was beaten up by four guys who didn't appreciate being a part of his conspiracy theories. He told me it took all four of them to get him, which I believe to be accurate. After I picked him up when he had a brief rest in our local hospital with a CAT Scan in the books, I never felt so sorry for a buddy in my life. No matter what I did to help him, it didn't stop his erratic behavior.

I made several trips up to Unionville with his son Brett and my son Josh. We all went back to Graceland to show the boys where it all started and met up with several old teammates. Although we were hours away, I texted or talked to him regularly. His overall demeanor was not like the Eric I had known after he returned home, but he always wanted the best for his kids and wanted them to know how much he loved them. He would tell me this every time we talked. He also knew how much everyone loved him as well, as I always conveyed this to him. He knew how important he was not only to his kids, but to all of our friends and families.

When Eric's parents called me to write a short chapter about Eric's life in a book about suicide, I went temporarily numb. I never actually knew how my friend died. I had suspicions, but never asked about any details. I was comforted by the fact that I knew he wasn't mentally or physically hurting anymore. I watched him suffer and I will never be able to convey how much on paper. The demons in his head were too much for the feistiest man I have ever met. In this same year, a favorite football player of mine, Junior Seau committed suicide and CTE became a heavily discussed problem with football players. Chronic

Traumatic Encephalopathy is my formal diagnosis for my friend. I know the only way this is diagnosed is with post-mortem brain tissue samples, but my buddy had not only a history of head trauma, but developed almost every symptom associated with this disease. He had memory loss, confusion, impaired judgment, impulse control problems, aggression, depression, suicidality, parkinsonism and eventually progressive dementia.

I will never forget my last conversation with Eric. He was excited about watching a new show about to start called *Duck Dynasty,* and felt that I needed to make sure and watch, and he told me to listen to a song by George Strait called "Troubadour." I did both and still think of him all of the time. I'm sure when we meet again, something is going to get torn up as it did when we first met!

CHAPTER 11

POST CONCUSSION SYNDROME AND CHRONIC TRAUMATIC ENCEPHALOPATHY

BEFORE CHRONIC TRAUMATIC ENCEPHALOPATHY, THERE IS POST CONCUSSION SYNDROME

The experts at *Theraspecs* tell us that following a concussion (also known as mild traumatic brain injury), many people experience lasting symptoms in what is often referred to as "Post Concussion Syndrome" (PCS) (TheraSpecs, 2019). However, the symptoms themselves can manifest in different ways for different patients, which makes PCS particularly difficult to diagnose.

According to *Cognitive Fx*, a concussion is a mild traumatic brain injury (TBI), which is a change in brain function caused by force to the head or body. This can happen in sports, car accidents, falling, or anything similar. A concussion can even be the result of whiplash. Whenever the body moves quickly back and forth and the brain hits the inside of the skull, it can result in a concussion. A concussion can cause damage to nerves and neurons; it can alter the blood flow in the brain and cause chemical and functionality change in the brain.

Both Post Concussion Syndrome and Chronic Traumatic Encephalopathy are considered neurological disorders which are long-term effects of concussion(s). While both can have similar symptoms, it is important to note the differences between them:

According to the experts at Theraspecs, the symptoms of PCS that continue after an injury can include (TheraSpecs, 2019):

PHYSICAL SYMPTOMS

- Headaches and migraines rank as one of the most common complaints affecting as many as 90% of patients at all stages of the condition.

These headaches can last anywhere from three to six months to over a year. Dizziness and vertigo, fatigue, sensitivity to light, blurred vision and noise are also symptoms.

COGNITIVE SYMPTOMS

- difficulty concentrating

- memory loss

- delayed/slow thinking

EMOTIONAL SYMPTOMS

- anxiety

- depression

- sleep disturbances

Post Concussion Syndrome is real and can be diagnosed by a healthcare professional. It can be treated. Its counterpart, Chronic Traumatic Encephalopathy (CTE) is also real, but cannot be diagnosed until after death with a brain biopsy. There is no known test to diagnose someone with CTE. Treatment of CTE may be geared towards reducing the symptoms rather than fixing the brain.

CHRONIC TRAUMATIC ENCEPHALOPATHY

A few weeks after Eric's funeral, a good friend of his stopped by to see us. We were discussing how Eric had changed, how paranoid he had become, and that we knew there was something wrong but we could not find the answers to help him. She told us, "When Eric was in college, he would often call me after a ballgame and tell me how bad his head was hurting and that he couldn't get it to stop."

"Eric complained of a headache every morning when he got up," Bob recalls, "But I just thought it was his allergies. I now wonder if it could have been something worse, even that far back."

It doesn't matter if your child is three years old or forty-three years old, if they were suffering from cancer or some other life-threatening disease, you would try to find the best doctors there are to help them.

We don't know exactly how many head injuries Eric had throughout his high school and college years, but we do know it was many. We also learned he had a really bad fall, hitting the back of his head when skating with his kids. He would often refuse to see a doctor, but for the times he did and for the tests they performed, we don't feel that they knew what to look for.

"Imagine hitting your head so hard you begin seeing stars, the room starts spinning, and you feel like you are going to vomit—then everything goes black. These are a few of the symptoms individuals who suffer a concussion will often experience, including headaches, confusion, nausea, vomiting, dizziness and even losing consciousness. What if there is a brain disease with far worse effects then a concussion and can even lead to death?

Many of the symptoms of CTE are not as obvious as the symptoms patients experience with a concussion, and these symptoms typically do not begin until years after the initial head injuries. These symptoms tend to worsen over time and can lead to dementia.

The majority of known cases of CTE have occurred in athletes who participated in contact sports such as football,

*hockey, soccer, boxing, and wrestling. Other risk factors for
the condition include being in the military, domestic violence,
and repeated hitting of the head. The exact amount of trauma
that creates the condition is unknown for now and the
diagnosis of CTE occurs by examining a patient's brain tissue
during an autopsy.*

*Chronic Traumatic Encephalopathy is caused by multiple
head injuries which are often substantial blows to the head
with some leading to concussions. However, concussions are
not what triggers this disease. The disease is distinguished by
abnormal deposits of calcium of proteins throughout the brain.
Researchers have observed abnormal buildup of the protein tau,
which kills brain cells and is a signifier of CTE"* (L'Ecuyler).

Chronic Traumatic Encephalopathy is now being
acknowledged because of the attention athletes, especially
football players, have received in the last few years and the
research now being done to help those who suffer from it.

Research shows that people with CTE may be at an
increased risk of suicide. For those who are so depressed
they believe the only relief from their pain is to commit
suicide, then they have reached a point where they have
slipped out of reality and into their own dark world of
confusion and pain.

According to Theraspecs, there are four major categories
of symptoms for Chronic Traumatic Encephalopathy
(TheraSpecs, 2019):

MOOD CHANGES

- depression

- helplessness

- anxiety

- apathy

- rage

BEHAVIOR

- short fuse

- aggression

- poor impulse control

- violence

COGNITIVE FUNCTION

- inability to remember

- forgetting new information quickly

- poor executive functions such as planning, organizational, multitasking, judgment

MOTOR FUNCTION

- most commonly seen in boxers: tremors, gait, balance

We identified Eric two ways: "Good Eric" and "Bad Eric." "Good Eric" was calm and would stop by to eat supper with us; he would talk about his work and his children. He was probably the best "Good Eric" when his children would come to visit him. They would invite their cousins to come and enjoy the lake activities with them, such as swimming, fishing and barbecuing and for a little while, he seemed almost normal.

We totally understand how frightening it must have been for Eric's wife and children when he was living at home with "Bad Eric". The turmoil and fear that followed his irrational behavior must have been upsetting. His son was 13 and his daughter was 11 when he committed suicide, so they were very young when he became ill. Their lives, as they then knew them, changed dramatically. Seeing your father change the way Eric did had to be terrible and at times, very scary.

CHAPTER 12

SUICIDE: A PUBLIC HEALTH CRISIS

The following information was taken from a column dated July 17, 2005 by Ron Rolheiser, OMI—speaker, columnist, and author, and used with his permission:

"Suicide, no doubt, is the most misunderstood of all deaths and leaves behind a residue of questions, guilt, anger, second-guessing, and anxiety which, at least initially, is almost impossible to digest. Suicide, at least in most cases, is a sickness, a disease, a terminal illness that takes a person out of life, as does any terminal illness, against his or her will. In essence, suicide is death through emotional cancer, emotional heart attack, emotional stroke. That's why it's apt to say that someone is a "victim of suicide". Suicide is a desperate, if misguided attempt to end unendurable pain at any cost; suicide is an illness. To lose a loved one to death is painful, to lose a loved one to suicide is also disorienting"
(Rolheiser).

There is no blueprint for how we react to and cope after the death of a loved one. We each grieve in our own way and at our own pace. When someone grieves in a different way than us, it doesn't mean they "don't care," they are just finding their own way to cope *(Survivors of Bereavement by Suicide).*

For some, losing a loved one to suicide causes them to question their faith in God and blame him for what happened. I don't think any of us ever felt that way. I know Bob and I didn't; if anything, it made our faith stronger.

The *Missouri Institute of Mental Health* reported in 2018: "In Missouri, suicide is the 10th leading cause of death, making Missouri the 14th ranked state in the nation with a rate of 18.33 (per 100,000, age-adjusted)".[1] The national rate is 13.42 deaths by suicide per 100,000 population. Twice as many people died by suicide than by homicide.[2] Over 1,000 Missourians died by suicide in 2016

[1]University of Missouri—Saint Louis. *Missouri Institute of Mental Health.* "Suicide Prevention: facts and resources in Missouri." 2018.
[2]©2019 United Health Foundation. All Rights Reserved.

(*Missouri Department of Mental Health, 2016*). Between 1999 and 2016, the suicide rate in Missouri rose by over 30%.[2] Putnam County, the rural Missouri county we live in with a population of less than 5000, is ranked #26 out of 114 counties for suicide deaths".

In 2016, those who died by suicide were 76% male and 92% were Caucasian. Fifty seven percent of all suicides in 2016 involved firearms followed by suffocation (24%) and poisoning (14%). [3]

Suicide has become a large public health crisis. The legislature needs to recognize this and focus on how serious this problem is and that it is not going away. According to statistics, it is only getting worse. More needs to be done to help with this growing health crisis.

A 96-hour hold should be just that. No one should be released until their 96 hours are up. A doctor needs to communicate with the family to get the information they need to fully understand the patient and the problems they have been experiencing. There must be more treatment centers and professionals who are qualified in treating patients with a mental illness.

WHERE WE STAND NATIONALLY

According to the latest information from *American Foundation For Suicide Prevention (AFSP)*, in 2017 roughly around 47,000 Americans died by suicide—a person dies by suicide every 12.8 minutes. Suicide is the 10th leading cause of death in the United States.[1] On average, 129 suicides occur per day and firearms account for 51% of all suicides.[2] White males accounted for 69.67% of suicide deaths in 2017.[2]

In the US, there are no complete counts of suicide available. *The Center for Disease and Control* gathers information from hospitals for injuries or self-harm. In

[3] Information courtesy of the Missouri Department of Mental Health.

2015—the most recent data—575,000 people visited a hospital for self-harm. It is believed that rates are actually higher than what is reported. Only half of all Americans experiencing an episode of Major Depression receive treatment.

A 2017 national survey of drug use and mental health estimated that 0.6% of adults, age 18 and older, made at least one suicide attempt. This translates to approximately 1.4 million adults. Men died by suicide three and half time times more often than women. Twice as many people died by suicide than by homicide. Total deaths to suicide reflect a total of 24,274 years of potential life lost before age 65. There is one successful suicide for every 25 suicide attempts.

The suicide rate rose in all states but one between 1999 and 2016, with increases seen across age, gender, race, and ethnicity. In more than one-half of all deaths in 27 states, the people had no known mental health condition when they ended their life. Suicide rates went up more than 30% in half of the states since 1999.[2]

The following warning signs of suicide are indicators that a person may be in acute danger and may urgently need help:

- talking about wanting to die or to kill oneself

- looking for a way to kill oneself/such as searching on line or buying a gun

- talk about feeling hopeless or having no reason to live

- talking about feeling trapped or unbearable pain

- talking about being a burden to others

- increasing use of alcohol or drugs

- acting anxious or agitated; behaving recklessly

- sleeping too much or too little

- withdrawing or feeling isolated

- showing rage or talking about seeking revenge

- displaying extreme mood swings

- losing interest in things, or losing the ability to experience pleasure

The above information is from the *American Suicide Prevention*.

WHAT LEADS TO SUICIDE?

There is no single cause for suicide. Suicide most often occurs when stressors and health issues converge to create an experience of hopelessness and despair. Conditions like depression, anxiety, and substance abuse problems (especially when unaddressed) increase the risk for suicide. It is important to note that most people who actively manage their mental health conditions go on to engage in life.

- Over 50% of all people who die by suicide suffer from Major Depression.

- If one includes alcoholics who are depressed, this figure rises to over 75%.

- Depression affects nearly 5-8% of Americans ages 18 and over in a given year.

- More Americans suffer from depression than coronary heart disease, cancer, and HIV/AIDS. Between 80% and 90% of people with depression respond positively to treatment and almost all patients gain some relief from their symptoms. But first, depression has to be recognized.

The American Foundation for Suicide Prevention tells us, if you think someone is thinking about suicide, assume you are the only one who will reach out.

Have an honest conversation with them by:

- talking to them in private

- listen to their story

- tell them you care about them

- ask directly if they are thinking about suicide

- encourage them to seek treatment or to contact their doctor or therapist

- avoid debating the value of life, minimizing their problems or giving advice

If they say they are considering suicide:

- take them seriously and stay with them

- help them remove lethal means

- call the National Suicide Prevention Lifeline: 1-800-273-8255

- text TALK to 741741 to text with a trained counselor from the crisis text line for free 24/7

- escort them to mental health services or an emergency room

All of the above information is from the *American Suicide Prevention.*

Most people who take their lives exhibit one or more warning signs, either through what they say or what they do. When someone dies from suicide, family and friends are devastated. Those who take their lives do not realize how many more people would be devastated by their death—and how many more would be as affected. We are all different, do not worry that you are not reacting in the right or wrong way, we all respond differently to a death by suicide.

For a parent who is dealing with the suicide of a child, there are ideas to help you cope:

- Talk about your child's death with family members and discuss your feelings of loss and pain.

- Ask for help. Don't be afraid to let your friends know what you need when they ask; they want to help.

- Consider becoming involved with a self-help bereavement group

- Give yourself time, time, and more time. It takes months, even years to open your heart and mind to healing. Choose to survive and then be patient with yourself. In time, your grief will soften as you begin to heal and you will feel like investing in life again.

CHAPTER 13

THE END OF A JOURNEY

This part of our journey is now complete. Writing this book was a step in our healing process. Even though our pain from losing Eric will never end, we do what we can to be at peace with it.

We want everyone to know the kind of person Eric was and that he committed suicide because he was very, very sick. To see our son, brother, father, husband, friend and teammate change the way Eric did was hard for all of us. If someone like Eric, who "would have been the last person to commit suicide," could get to the point that he was not in control of his thoughts, emotions, and actions, then it can happen to anyone.

Those who have never suffered from Major Depression cannot fully understand the pain that it causes to the one who is enveloped in its curse. For some, it is hard to understand why those who suffer from depression cannot "just get over it." If it were only that easy. But it is not; medication and counseling can sometimes help, but they may not always be enough.

Our hearts break when we remember the physical and mental pain Eric was feeling. We feel the hopelessness of being unable to free him of that agony. To see our grown son cry because he was so consumed by pain and by sadness, that he had lost his will to keep living broke our hearts. When he was a child, we could wipe his tears, tell him everything is going to be okay, and know that it would be. But as a grown man, we could have told him this but we all knew it wasn't true.

A mother and father that hold their newborn child for the first time do not see a future where that child will grow up to commit suicide. The future they see is a bright one full of sunshine, rainbows, and laughter. You don't want to think of the "what ifs" or the pain and suffering the newborn might one day feel. You only want the best, and you try hard to be a good parent. But there are some things that are out of our control; and the good, healthy, and happy life you envision for that newborn may be far different from the one he or she ends up living. You can't always do everything you want to do to change your loved one's life.

As parents, Bob and I worried about our children having a car wreck, getting life-threatening illnesses, or being murdered. But never, never in a million years, did we ever think that one of them would commit suicide.

As we already said in this story, suicide has become a public health crisis and the increase in suicides is very worrisome. What can we do to prevent suicide?

The Center for Disease and Control offers the following suggestions:

1. States can help ease unemployment and housing stress.

2. Healthcare can offer treatment options by phone or online services.

3. Employers can apply policies that create a healthy work environment.

4. Communities can offer informative programs and events.

5. Schools can teach students skills to manage life's challenges.

6. Media can describe helping resources and avoid headlines or details that increase risk.

For parents who are worried about their child playing contact sports and the role head injuries could possibly play regarding their mental health later in life, we cannot stress enough to be very watchful of any head injury your child receives. Do not think it was "not a hard enough hit" to cause injury to the brain or to cause a concussion. As we found out from our study on Post Concussion Syndrome and Post Traumatic Encephalopathy, patients who have experienced head trauma may have symptoms for as long as an entire year and possibly beyond. For individuals sustaining mild traumatic brain injuries (PCS), it can be diagnosed by a professional and can be treated. Chronic Traumatic Encephalopathy cannot be treated because there is no known test to diagnose CTE and treatment may be geared towards reducing the symptoms rather than fixing the brain. Both PCS and CTE are very real and very dangerous.

Find out about the sports equipment your child uses and make sure it is sufficient; be persistent if necessary. Do your homework and if what you find is not satisfactory, if the equipment is not as good as it should be, then make your voice heard until you get what is needed to protect them. It could just save their life down the road. We wish when our children were young and playing sports that we knew then what we know now; maybe things would have turned out differently for Eric.

For those of us that knew Eric when he was young (when he was happy, healthy, full of life, and would have given you the shirt off his back) we will always remember him that way. He would not want us to remember him the way he was at the end.

He loved his wife and children so much. The last thing he would have wanted to do would be to cause them any unhappiness or pain. He knew there was something wrong with him; did he know it could possibly be CTE and that he would never get better, only worse? Did he think that committing suicide was the only way he had to protect his family from himself?

After seven years of crying, one would think that there could not possibly be any tears left. I feel certain that in seven more years there will be more tears. Time will not define the amount of tears a heartbroken father, mother, brother, sister, son, daughter, wife, and friend will cry.

A family is like a chain, with each link connecting to the next to make it strong and complete. When you lose a loved one, that link is gone and cannot be replaced. The chain is no longer complete, but you have to try and keep it together and keep it strong the best way you can.

We often wonder: *If Eric would have given life one more day what might have happened?* One more day could have been the day we found the help he needed. One more day could have been the day that a cure was found for his mental illness or a cure for CTE. One more day could have been the day his pain was gone—one more day; just one more day.

We hope all who are contemplating committing suicide will stop and think that tomorrow could be that one more day. Do not end your life today when tomorrow or the next tomorrow could be the day that ends your suffering. Never, never give up on today in hopes for tomorrow.

We so wish we had one more day with Eric. Maybe one more day or one more tomorrow could have made the difference for him. We know Eric would be happy if sharing his story helps one person and we feel certain he would tell you to give your life a chance.

Life is a journey, and we don't know where that journey may take us next. We need to embrace life and our loved ones as if it is our last day with them because we never know when our last day may be. We have many beautiful memories of a special little boy who grew up to be a very special man.

Grieving is personal and sometimes we just need to be alone to cry, to pray, and to reflect on our memories. They are all we have left of our son and there are times when we don't want to share him with anyone.

We know that the greatest gift God gave us was our children. The greatest task He put before us was to raise those children. We are so thankful we had Eric for 43 years. He was a wonderful son and we would not have wanted to miss one minute we had with him. Losing Eric is the greatest pain God is helping us to endure.

ACKNOWLEDGEMENTS

DR. JOCELYN CULLITY

Director of the BFA in Creative Writing program at Truman State University. Professor Cullity is the reason our dream of writing this book became a reality. She put her knowledge and expertise on a personal level to help make a difficult and painful task easier. We will never be able to thank her enough.

TRUMAN STATE UNIVERSITY

We would also like to thank the following for all their excellent and essential help:

RUSTY NELSON, PROFESSOR OF ART

for his cover design

MARY SHAPIRO, CHAIR, DEPARTMENT OF ENGLISH AND LINGUISTICS

for Dr. Shapiro's and the department's kind support of this community project

ASHLEY BURGESS, STUDENT

for her design work

BETSY AND NEAL DELMONICO

for giving us our ISBN, and for so much other valuable book information

GENE WEECE

Senior Minister at the First Christian Church in Unionville, MO. He was always there for us knowing the right things to say to help us survive the worst pain a mother and father can ever experience. He helped us to realize that we needed to use our story to help others.

KARLA KLINGNER DIAZ

Guided us through the legal part of Eric's estate with love and compassion in what could have otherwise been a heart-wrenching ordeal. We will always remember her kindness, compassion and professionalism.

OUR FRIENDS

near and far for their love, concern, and for always being there for us

THE COMMUNITY WE LIVE IN

for their continuing love and support

REFERENCES

American Foundation For Suicide Prevention (2020).

Cognitive Fx. (2020). "Post-Concussion Treatment Center."
www.cognitivefxusa.com.

L'Ecuyer, Danielle. "What is CTE And How Is It Related To Concussions?" HealthPrep.com, Pub Labs International, Inc, 19 January 2018, https://healthprep.com/conditions/cte-and-concussions/.

Missouri Department of Health: Division of Behavioral Health.(2018). "Missouri Assessment of College Health Behaviors."

Missouri Department of Mental Health. (2016). "Missouri Student Survey."

National Survey of Drug Use and Health (2019). www.samhsa.gov/data/sites/default/files/cbhsq-reports/NSDUHNationalFindingsReport2018.pdf

Pub Labs International, Inc. (2018). healthprep.com/conditions/cte-and-concussions.

Rolheiser, Fr. Ron. *The Oblate School.* "The Struggle To Understand Suicide." Currently,Father Rolheiser is serving as President of the Oblate School of Theology in San Antonio, Texas. He can be contacted through his website, www.ronrolheiser.com.

Survivors of Bereavement by Suicide. (2020). www.uksobs.org.

*The Compassionate Friends: supporting a family
after a loved one dies.*
(2020). www.compassionatefriends.org.

TheraSpecs,(2019). https://www.theraspecs.com
/blog/symptoms-post-concussion-syndrome/

University of Missouri—Saint Louis. (2018).
Missouri Institute of Mental Health. "Suicide
Prevention: facts and resources in Missouri."

United Health Foundation.(2020).
www.americashealthrankings.org.

US Department of Health and Human Services. (2020).
Center for Disease Control. www.cdc.gov.

World Life Expectancy. (2018).
www.worldlifeexpectancy.com.